STOP &
SHIFT

KAREN ALLEN

Published and Distributed by
SOUND WISDOM
PO Box 310
Shippensburg, PA 17257-0310
717-530-2122
info@soundwisdom.com
www.soundwisdom.com

While efforts have been made to verify information contained in this publication, neither the author nor the publisher assumes any responsibility for errors, inaccuracies, or omissions. While this publication is chock-full of useful, practical information, it is not intended to be legal or accounting advice. All readers are advised to seek competent lawyers and accountants to follow laws and regulations that may apply to specific situations. The reader of this publication assumes responsibility for the use of the information. The author and publisher assume no responsibility or liability whatsoever on the behalf of the reader of this publication.

ISBN 13 TP: 978-1-64095-382-6
ISBN 13 eBook: 978-1-64095-383-3

For Worldwide Distribution, Printed in the U.S.A.
 2 3 4 5 6 / 26 25 24 23

TO MY SON, CALEB—

Everything I do is for you.
I pray that you always stay connected to your true self
and never forget that you are a magnificent, powerful being of light.
I love you to the other galaxies and back, times twelve.

**TO ALL OF THE BEAUTIFUL HUMANS WHO WANT
TO MAKE THIS WORLD A BETTER PLACE—**

Remember, change starts within you.
I hope after reading this book you feel empowered
to become the YOU you always intended to be.

CONTENTS

" In every moment, of every day, you have the power to choose how you're going to respond to life."

1

Wait, You Don't Want to Miss This!

If you don't believe you have the power to change your thoughts and control your choices, then this book isn't for you. I'm just giving you a fair warning right here on page one because I don't want you to waste your time.

If you're sticking around—welcome, my friend. We have one rule in this space: no raggedy excuses. None of that "But Karen, you don't understand..." or "You don't know what I've been through..." stuff is allowed.

I know life is hard—trust me, I do. Not only is it hard; a lot of times, it's unfair! I hate to break it to you, but there will always be challenging moments and circumstances that are out of our control. The good news is we hold the power to shape our lives when we mindfully choose our responses to those scenarios.

We think, we choose, we create.

No matter what the situation may be, you can redefine, rebuild, or reshape your life with your mind. I don't mean like in a superhero way, where you stare at an object and morph it with your brainpower. I'm talking about *intentional decision-making.* You're free to make choices about which words you speak, what actions you take, and how you focus your attention. Basically, you take control of your life by taking control of your mind.

I remember watching an interview with Oprah Winfrey where she put it perfectly. She said, "You are responsible for your life. If you're waiting around for somebody to save you, fix you, to even help you, you are wasting your time. Because only you have the power to move your life forward."[1]

Yeesh! That hits the heart. That's one of those undeniable truths that no one can argue. And it doesn't just sound good; I know this to be true from my own personal experience.

Let me rewind a bit to give you my backstory…

I should give you a warning first. My story is one that makes people respond with some variation of "Oh my God, that's horrible!" And they're right—it *is* horrible. When I step out of my shoes and look at my life from an outsider's perspective, it seriously looks like a sad and shocking Lifetime movie.

Which, for the record, wouldn't be my choice for the genre of my life. I'd love to have a sweet Hallmark-movie life, where there's only a little drama but nothing that can't be resolved with a kiss and some snow. But unfortunately, my movie is much more of a heartbreaking mystery than a quaint romance.

Ready? Here it goes…

When I was 29 years old, my husband was murdered.

Yes, you read that correctly.

That Monday started off like any other. I was at work, recruiting for a critical high-level position. I'd been on the phone with candidates all day, and a few of the interviews needed to be scheduled for after office hours. So I texted my husband, Richard, and told him that I was going to have to make some calls from home that evening.

At the time, Rich was a newly established CrossFit gym owner. He'd opened the gym six months earlier on his birthday weekend, in March 2013, and in those few months since the grand opening, business had grown quickly. It was an exciting and busy time for our family. We really had the teamwork thing down pat. You know how a relay team has to pass off the baton smoothly to one another while running their race to keep pace? That was us.

Rich would start his morning super early because his first class of the day was at 6:30 a.m. I'd often wake up to a text or a sweet note on a Post-it stuck to the door of the microwave. I'd get the kids up, fed, dressed, and out the door, dropping off our son, Caleb, at the gym before taking my stepdaughter to school. During the summer, however, Rich was full-blown daddy day care with both of the kids at the gym. Although he was focused on growing his business, he loved having his kids around—they were his pride and joy.

On this particular day, I texted to tell him about the interviews I had to do from home that evening and asked if he wanted me to come get the kids or if they wanted to stay with him. We arranged for me to pick them up from the gym, where they'd been with him all day.

On my way there, I received a phone call from work regarding the candidates we were interviewing. When I pulled into the parking lot, I was still on the phone with the hiring manager, so Richard quickly loaded the kids in the car. We waved goodbye, and I drove away.

That was the last time I ever saw my husband alive.

I dropped off my stepdaughter at her mom's house. My two-year-old and I headed home so I could get him settled with dinner and distracted with the Disney Channel before hopping on my first interview of the evening.

I grabbed the house phone, silenced my cell phone, sat at our dining-room table, and dialed the first candidate promptly at our scheduled time.

About halfway through the call (remember, this is back in the day when we conducted interviews primarily on the phone and not through our computer screens), while going through my standard interview questions with the applicant, I noticed my cell phone buzzing. It was face down, so I couldn't see who was calling. At first, I didn't think anything of it, but after a couple of minutes of nonstop vibrations, I turned it over to see that I had several missed calls from one of our members at the gym.

You know how we can think a million thoughts in a millisecond? That's exactly what happened at that moment. At first I was thinking, *Richard must have fallen off the rig…maybe he broke his arm.*

But then I thought, *No, he must have hit his head, because if he broke his arm, he'd still call. He's such a tough guy.*

Just as I asked the candidate another question, my cell started buzzing again. When he launched into his response, I quickly put him on mute so I could answer the call, and as soon as I did, all I could hear was screaming.

People in the background were yelling, and the friend who called me was hysterical. Finally, I could make out a single word: "Shot."

Immediately—and I do mean *immediately*—my body started convulsing. While I was trying to process what she'd just told me, I darted to the bedroom, walked into our closet, and tried to gather myself without Caleb seeing me in a total panic.

In a matter of seconds, I had to figure out what to do next, where to take Caleb, whom to call…and then I realized that the candidate was still on mute!

With my heart pounding, body shaking, and mind in utter chaos, I had to try to calm the quiver in my voice so I could take the candidate off mute and say, "Thank you so much for your time. We'll be in contact with the next steps."

I hung up as fast as I could.

I ran back downstairs and picked up my son. I couldn't find the words to explain what was going on. So instead, I gently bounced him in my arms, because I didn't want him to feel the convulsions that were ripping through my body. I rushed over to our neighbors' house, banged on their door, and asked them to watch Caleb for a few hours.

As I jumped into the car, it dawned on me that I still had two more interviews scheduled that were most definitely not going to happen. I called my boss to tell him what was going on. He could hear the panic in my voice and insisted on staying on the phone with me to make sure I arrived at the gym safely.

Once I got on the highway, I was flying, going 100-plus miles per hour. Then, my phone started blowing up. The news traveled like wildfire, time felt like it was moving at warp speed, and my thoughts were all over the place.

As I pulled up to the light right before our gym, I thought to myself, *Wait wait wait, why am I not on my way to the hospital? It's been a while since I got the first call. They would have rushed him to the hospital, right?*

Then I turned the corner to the gym, and all I could see was complete pandemonium. There were local news vans and reporters. First responders. People from our church. People from the community. People I knew, others I didn't. It was straight-up chaos.

I jumped out of my car and into a harsh reality I wasn't prepared to face—I was told that an unidentified person walked into our CrossFit and shot my husband three times while he was teaching his class. Reality blurred and everything ran together until I could barely breathe. I don't remember who told me my husband didn't survive, but I do remember they told me that he died instantly.

All I could do at that point was crouch behind a bush and rock back and forth, repeating to myself, "This isn't real. This isn't real. This isn't real."

I wasn't allowed to go anywhere near the gym because by the time I arrived, the police had most of the parking lot already roped off and the forensic team was on the hunt for any clues. When I got a glimpse of them rolling the black body bag into the back of an ambulance, I still couldn't comprehend that my husband, to whom I'd just waved goodbye a few hours earlier, was dead.

After lingering around the crime scene for several hours, waiting and hoping for instant answers, I finally headed home around 1:30 a.m. I was shocked, afraid, confused, angry, *all* the things…

That night changed the trajectory of my life—forever. The next year was pure hell as I sought answers and didn't get them. (Even now, years later, I still don't have closure to his case. "It went cold," as they say.)

So yes, friend, I know that life can be hard and unfair, and I know what it feels like to have the wind knocked out of you. But I also know we're not defined by our hard times.

Let me say it a different way: *YOU are NOT defined by what's happened to you.* You are defined by what you do. And your character is defined by how you respond to the things that try to break you. I know this is true because I have walked that road. I have used tools to build resilience and to rise up to meet life's challenges. So I know without a doubt in my mind that you can use these tools too.

Now, before I share the redemptive part of this story, let me first admit that I hate it when people try to console a brokenhearted friend with, "Everything happens for a reason."

> You are not defined by what's happened to you. You are defined by what you do.

Cue the eye roll.

It's one of the most insensitive things to say to someone who's completely devastated—and it creates a false sense of closure. (There are some pretty terrible things that happen in this world for which we may never find the "closure" we crave.) However, that doesn't make that statement *un*true. It's just unhelpful to those battling through it.

The "reason" is actually revealed by our response. And the key is to be open to the opportunity to grow through the pain instead of choosing to be held back by anger, bitterness, or misery. The hard truth is, we may never know the "why" behind every life event or circumstance, but we can find purpose in these difficulties if, and only if, we consciously choose our response.

That perspective helped shape my journey. As a matter of fact, there's a fancy scientific term for it: post-traumatic growth. First theorized by two psychologists, Richard Tedeschi and Lawrence Calhoun, post-traumatic growth (PTG) refers to the positive personal transformation that people can experience following trauma.

This concept first emerged in the mid-1990s when Tedeschi and Calhoun identified five expressions of PTG: enhanced personal strength, newfound appreciation of life, deeper interpersonal relationships, spiritual growth, and increased ability to see new possibilities.[2]

I didn't even know this existed until I read Sheryl Sandberg and Adam Grant's book *Option B*. When I read that "in the wake of most crushing blows, people can find greater strength and deeper meaning," I realized, *Whoa, I'm not crazy! That natural growth feeling is a THING!*[3]

You should've seen my face. It was like someone just told me that all my debt had been paid off. It was an immense, enthusiastic sense of relief to discover post-traumatic growth. Learning this term helped me release the guilt that came with moving forward. It unlocked more space in my mind to grieve and grow at the same time. Instead of wrestling with my pain and feeling weighed down by it, I could embrace it, learn from it, and use it to fuel my growth.

If I could describe the experience of studying this concept to you in one word it would be—freedom.

I adopted the belief that everything in life is an access point for growth, which helped me realize there's no need to fight or resent the unwanted emotions. You liberate yourself by reshaping animosity into curiosity.

I'm so grateful I was able to fully adopt this mindshift—or life wouldn't be what it is now. Today, despite the trauma I've experienced and the many setbacks that have tried to steal my peace, I am the happy, healthy, whole mom that I set out to be, and because of that, my son and I are both thriving. Anyone who knows me knows that this was, is, and always will be my number-one priority.

> Liberate yourself by reshaping animosity into curiosity.

I discovered routines that support my energy, created new habits to protect my inner peace, and most importantly, I've done the work to heal and overcome the grimy depths of grief. Heck, I *still* do the work, because I don't think we ever stop grieving; I think we just learn how to manage it in our lives.

I gave a TEDx talk—that was an incredible experience.

I built a six-figure speaking business.

I've had the honor of working with amazing clients like Golf Channel, Google, YouTube, Universal Parks & Resorts Orlando, Wawa, Kaiser Permanente, HDR, HubSpot, Lockheed Martin, GAP, Inc., and so many more!

I expanded my speaking business and began helping companies implement wellness strategies to create workplaces where people can thrive.

I don't say any of this to brag. I'm sharing my truth because I hope it inspires you to take control of your mindset and, more importantly, make life beautiful in the mess. In the midst of any trial, setback, or any number of life's disruptions, you can face your troubles and *grow* from them. Growth can be a generous gift, and good news—the struggle is not required. You don't have to go through a painful experience to level up your life; you just need to choose to grow.

Operating from this new perspective is what enabled me to carefully consider my response to such an unthinkable tragedy. It also provided the pathway that my heart and mind needed to properly heal. Mastering my thoughts helped me respond to injustice, hate, fear, and anxiety without losing gratitude, hope, and courage. Learning how to catch my negative thoughts and reshape them has empowered me to remain steadfast in love and peace despite this harsh, unpredictable, and unfair world in which we live.

You have the ability to choose what you fill your life with. Do you want to fill it with things that are stressful, or do you want to fill it with things that are peaceful? Dragging around guilt, bitterness, and hopelessness is unhealthy and, not to mention, pointless. No good comes from this. I mean, let's be real—no one actually wants to go through life feeling low and unfulfilled.

But often it's the little things compounding over time that wear us down because we keep dwelling on them. Or it's past experiences that we haven't been able to let go of that leave us overwhelmed, fearful, and sad. The goal is to learn to deal with real feelings in a productive way. If you don't, you'll start to experience an internal buildup. Feelings and frustrations that are stored up inside create a blockage that prevents you from being in flow. Before you know it, you'll find yourself in a quicksand funk, and if you aren't careful, you can slip into a deep depression.

My hope is that after reading this book and learning the *Stop & Shift* method, you will renew your mind with carefully crafted choices so you can live a rich, full, authentic life.

This technique will help you make better decisions not driven by heightened emotions or ego, but instead shaped by quality thoughts and choices. This is without a doubt the best foundation for a healthy, happy life. *Stop & Shift* will improve your thinking and choices, which ultimately improves everything your life touches.

If you're ready to let go of everything that's holding you back from living fully, then let's get this journey started! Are you with me?

Let's *Stop & Shift*.

*" A quiet mind is able to
hear intuition over fear,
clarity over chaos,
and peace over grief. "*

2

Discovering *Stop & Shift*

Becoming a widow is like being automatically inducted into a secret society that no one wants to be a part of, and being a *young* widow is especially isolating. My peers couldn't understand the weight of my sadness because they couldn't relate to this type of loss. Plus, it was hard for me to find the words to describe the battle that was raging inside me.

Even with amazing friends and a loving family who were available and willing to support me through this, I felt terribly alone. I didn't want to burden others with my emotional baggage. I didn't want to ask for help. Heck, I could barely even think straight. However, one message kept emerging in my spirit: "You're going to take your pain, turn it into purpose, and pay it forward to help others."

I remember the first time I heard that in my soul, I was like, "Uhhh, nah… you've got the wrong girl! I have nothing to give to this world." But along the way I realized that if we were all more willing to share our stories—our real stories, not the curated ones on Instagram—it would help others feel less alone in their struggles and could fuel them with hope to keep growing forward.

Everyone's going through something; we all have our struggles. We've just been taught through societal norms not to share the messy parts of life and instead act like we have it all together. This is bullshit, and that's why I started sharing my story and teaching people the new tools and techniques I discovered along the way. And just to be clear, it doesn't have to be the death of a loved one that is weighing you down mentally and emotionally. It could be losing your job. It could be going through a divorce or healing from childhood trauma. It could just be feeling unfulfilled in life and carrying the burden of apathy. The details of our stories may be different, but I promise the *pain* is the same.

We find ourselves in a rough patch, and instead of taking responsibility for our healing, we tend to push it down and start operating on autopilot. I know because I've been there. When I was in the thick of my grief, I honestly wasn't looking for mindset techniques to save my life or change my circumstances; I was just trying to get through each day. At first, that was all I could do—and that was enough. But after a while, it felt empty and pointless. I realized that if I wanted to feel happy, healthy, and whole, I was going to have to do something, or *many* things, to make that happen.

So I shifted from autopilot to intentional living. I focused fundamentally on how to nurture my whole self: mental, emotional, physical, and spiritual. I didn't have a guide, I didn't take a course, and I couldn't afford therapy on a regular basis, so I just started doing what felt natural, with one goal in mind: decrease the risk of more suffering, negativity, and harm in our lives. This was my survival response. I knew my healing largely depended on my ability to protect my inner peace.

It started with little changes. One of the very first boundaries I established was that I no longer watched the news. Not that I was an avid news follower before Rich died, but I most definitely did NOT want to see my husband's name and our family photos flash across the morning and evening news with headlines like:

Local CrossFit owner shot and killed inside gym
Richard Millsap: slain CrossFit instructor
CrossFit Instructor shot dead in front of class

I also couldn't handle hearing details about what happened from the people who were there. So I protected my peace by removing myself from those conversations and leaving the room when necessary.

When the 911 calls were released, I remember a friend called me to ask if I'd listened to them. *Heck no!* Why would I want to relisten to the same distressed phone call I'd received from the gym member who called me when it *actually* happened? That would be like slicing open a recent wound that's trying to heal and pouring a gallon of gasoline on it. Pure torture.

I also didn't want the details of my husband's death discussed in front of our son. This was a healthy boundary for both of us; I wanted to protect his fragile little two-year-old mind from any graphic imagery that could be stimulated by hearing the story of how his dad died. When it came time to explain how it happened, I wanted to handle that delicate conversation with care.

So, as I consciously eliminated any source of bad energy, I became increasingly intentional about cultivating a peaceful, loving environment with good energy. And truth be told, I was so consumed with healing on purpose that I didn't even take time to reflect on my effort or take inventory of the practices that were making a significant impact. It wasn't until almost five years after Richard died, when my mom asked me, "What was the first thing you did to move past the pain and work toward your healing?" that I thought about it for a moment. I tried to trace back my efforts to a single choice—a moment in time—or a turning point.

As I traveled back in my head, it dawned on me. "I decided to change my mindset," I said. "I guess I just realized that I was either going to drive myself crazy and make myself sick, or I could try to turn my eyes away from the pain and focus on the present while being hopeful about the road ahead."

When we got off the phone, I couldn't shake her question. Our conversation got me thinking: *How can I explain this internal mindshift and share it with anyone else who feels stuck too?*

I checked my calendar to see what time my next meeting was and saw that I had enough time for a little meditation session. I put my phone on Do Not Disturb, set a timer on Alexa for twenty minutes, and lay down on the floor in my living room. I don't know what it is about lying down, but this is where I do my best clarity-work. As I started focusing on my breath, I remember thinking to myself: *How do I explain this thought process? What am I doing when I actively reframe my thoughts? What do I say?* Like I was trying to channel something from deep in my subconscious.

In that moment, I started to strongly visualize a time when I was able to turn from the most dominant negative thoughts. The thought that would drive me crazy the most—replaying how Richard died over and over again. Since I wasn't there when it happened, my thoughts would run all over the place with curiosity and fear...

Did he see it coming?
Was he scared?
Was he in pain?
What was his last thought?

All normal and natural thoughts, no doubt, but also an unhealthy space to live in for too long.

When those questions overpowered my mind, I forced myself to STOP thinking about the way he died and SHIFT my focus to the life he lived—all of the good things he did, the lives he touched, and the special and silly times we shared. I would literally walk myself through happy details like date nights or funny inside jokes and even ordinary moments like eating cake while watching reruns of *Martin* together. Now don't get me wrong—it would still hurt to think of him in the past tense, but it was better to focus on our love than on how his life was taken.

Lying there, the framework started flowing:

The very first step I take is to STOP the bad thought... Yes. That's exactly what I do. As soon as a negative thought tries to control me, I notice and release it. Turn from it immediately. Stop it dead in its tracks... And then what do I do? How do I move it in the right direction? I turn from it...but turn to what? I shift my eyes from bad to...SHIFT! I shift to something more positive and productive.

As this *Stop & Shift* method flooded my mind, I could think back to countless times when I'd been crying, highly stressed, feeling like I was drowning, and I'd gently shift those thoughts to something that would help pull me away from the impending breakdown.

I eventually started shifting to more hopeful thoughts of the future. I was very aware that my default state was mad, sad, and tired as hell. So I had to make a conscious decision: instead of fixating on all of the things that

> Permission to be honest? Just writing these words is taking me back to that place of sadness, deep suffering, and destructive thinking. I can feel the pain welling, and I'm reminded again why it's so dang important to train our minds not to dwell in negative spaces. *deep breath*

made me feel horrible, I would try and practice switching my thoughts to see hope for and faith in good things to come…even if I didn't believe it 100% at first. Sometimes believing only .01% is enough to get you through the negative thoughts and into a more positive mindset.

If you're reading this book, I know you already have some of that hope in you. You're probably not 100% sure that this technique is going to work for you, but trust me, just try it. That's what I did once I recognized the internal pattern. I kept trying it on, using it in simple day-to-day disruptions. I repeated *Stop & Shift* in my head. I ran through scenarios from my past. Over the next few weeks, I would find myself intentionally using the *Stop & Shift* method in any number of frustrating moments to see if it rang true. Then I shared it with a friend. Then a client. And another client. Then a class. And then on stages…and then in front of more audiences.

I credit my entire personal growth journey to the *Stop & Shift* technique. What you tell yourself on a daily basis, what you repeat in your mind, is more powerful than you know.

When I was just trying to make my way through my grief, I was following my gut, looking for things that brought me some relief. I didn't need to know why it worked. But now I understand that there was a ton of scientific evidence—and a whole branch of psychology—to explain why this mental exercise is so effective.

LET'S GET A LITTLE NERDY

Pardon me while I go all nerdy for a second…but what happens when you apply this technique is that you activate the prefrontal cortex, which is like the CEO of your brain. This area of the brain is in charge of decision-making, strategic thinking, acting with courage, learning new behaviors, and working toward goals. By activating the prefrontal cortex through the *Stop & Shift* method, you give yourself the mental space to find an alternate path. There are three key moments in this method: the pause, the internal reflection, and the conscious choice. Each step engages mindfulness, positive psychology, and neuroscience, which is a powerful combination for rewiring your brain and changing your life. Check it out…

Mindfulness helps you live in the moment. Not in your head, in the past, or in the future, but in the *now* so you can show up fully. In today's world, it's so easy to feel overwhelmed and like you're barely keeping up. But when you practice mindfulness, you learn how to focus your attention and build awareness of what's happening inside you and around you. When you're on a journey, it's always helpful to know where you're going, but the only thing that's *real* is the step you're taking at this very moment. I can't stress enough how important it is to make a habit of pausing to become more aware of the moment you're in. *Stop* is the pause, the practice of bringing yourself into the present moment so you can carefully choose how you want to show up.

Positive psychology is the scientific study of the strengths that enable individuals and communities to thrive. Research in this area has found that gratitude, social connection, and kindness are all important to living our best lives. To put it very simply: when you build on the good, the good gets better. Happiness, hope, grit—these aren't "nice-to-haves"; these can all be cultivated with practice. The *shift* part of the *Stop & Shift* exercise harnesses the power of positive psychology because the response you're choosing should be one that cultivates gratitude or kindness or other positive emotions and behaviors.

Neuroplasticity simply means your brain can change; it's moldable. What's the force that molds a brain? Experience. Our life experiences can reshape, change, and ultimately rewire our brains.

> When you build on the good, the good gets better.

When we encounter an event, our brain cells—neurons—become active, or "fire." The brain has billions of neurons, and each neuron has thousands of connections to other neurons. Everything that happens to us, and the way we respond to everything that happens to us, affects our brains. Your brain is constantly being wired and rewired based on your habits, your thoughts, and your life experiences. This is great news because it's a direct path to growth and transformation. When neurons fire together, they wire together. In other words, they grow new connections, and as they fire together again and again over time, these new connections lead to "rewiring" the brain. Every time you *stop* a negative thought cycle and *shift* to a more positive narrative, you're developing new neural connections.

We're going to dive in deeper in the following chapters, but for now, just know that you have the power to activate the part of your brain that will bring about positive change.

When you're up against a hardship or tragedy—*Stop & Shift*.
When you're battling negative self-talk—*Stop & Shift*.
When you want to make a major change in life—*Stop & Shift*.
When you desire clarity in life—*Stop & Shift*.
When you want to communicate better in a relationship—*Stop & Shift*.
When you need to bring calm to the chaos—*Stop & Shift*.
When you want to be a more present and patient parent—*Stop & Shift*.

TRAIN YOUR BRAIN

My husband was freakishly fit. No seriously, it was insane how many abs he had. Everyone would admire his ripped body, but what people didn't realize was how much he worked out! He played basketball five to six days a week for two to three hours a day before we opened the gym. Once he got CrossFit up and running, he spent less time playing ball and more time in the gym designing workouts for his clientele (he would never create a workout for his members without first doing it himself).

In short, this man was a beast. So if you see photos of his cut and chiseled muscles, keep in mind this is the result of hours of gym time. Richard's commitment to his health and physical well-being is a great metaphor for strategies that help us develop our mental strength.

The same way you do push-ups, sit-ups, and lift weights to get physically stronger, you can do mental exercises to build a healthy brain and strong mindset.

As a matter of fact, this is a great time to explain the umbrella of *mental wellness*. In the wake of the COVID-19 pandemic, we've had more vulnerable discussions at home and at work around mental health. This is great, but I think it's been pretty limited, and it's time to elevate the conversation. Most people shut down and stop listening when they hear the words "mental health" because they assume it pertains only to people with illnesses or disorders—which couldn't be further from the truth. That's like saying *only* people with high blood pressure or diabetes need to care for their physical health. Ridiculous, right?! Everyone needs to take care of their physical well-being, and everyone needs to take care of their mental well-being too.

Mental wellness includes mental *health*, but it also encompasses mental *strength* and mental *performance*—and practicing *Stop & Shift* has a positive impact on all three areas. I'm going to briefly break these down, but if you want more info, you should join the 100% Human community by signing up for my weekly newsletter, *Joy Bombs*, at www.karenallen.co. I share a ton of tips and resources to help you thrive mentally in all areas of life.

First, mental health is essentially brain health. Yes, some people have conditions or disorders influenced by a chemical imbalance in the brain that may require a treatment plan, but *all* humans need healthy habits to help their brain operate optimally. Getting enough sleep, drinking water, and even deep breathing are just a few daily practices that will make a significant impact on your mental health.

Then we have mental strength, which boils down to resilience and your ability to respond to disruptions with care. There are certain exercises we can practice that will help us develop our mental strength. For example, when you find yourself obsessively worrying about something, you can bring those heightened emotions into balance with logic. When you do this, it calms your nerves and re-engages the part of your brain that helps you think clearly—the prefrontal cortex. The more you practice balancing emotions with logic, the more you're building your mental strength.

And last, but of course not least, there's mental performance. Mental performance is probably the best-kept secret out here, seriously. Elite athletes like LeBron James, Serena Williams, and Michael Phelps have special trainers and consultants who specifically help them develop this area of mental wellness. Simply put, mental performance helps you tune out the noise and show up as your best self when the pressure is on. And it's not just for athletes. I mean, don't you want to show up as your best for that next presentation? Or when your kids are stressing you out, wouldn't be it great to have the tools to stay in flow? Mental performance isn't just something athletes need to learn; we all need these tools and skills.

When you train your brain and commit to your mental wellness, you improve your memory, focus, and overall functionality. I bet it would surprise you how many normal daily activities also offer brain-boosting benefits. Let me blow your mind for a second with this little fun fact: learning something new, solving a puzzle, taking deep breaths, being creative with arts and crafts, reading, and even dancing your heart out are all easy ways to stimulate brain activity and strengthen your mindset.

Stop & Shift is also an exercise to help strengthen and build new connections in your brain. Think of it as the burpee of mental fitness—challenging and sometimes even strenuous—but it produces major results! The more you shift, the more powerful your brain becomes.

Physical growth is easy to see because you're looking at developed muscles and a strong body. Internal growth is harder to see or measure because the progress isn't visible to the eye. But still, practice leads to progress, which leads to results. The end result is you thriving mentally with a healthy brain and clear mind. Notice I didn't say, "All of your problems will go away!" Sorry, friend, that's not possible. It's like the saying goes—"life doesn't get easier; you get stronger." So true.

YOU'RE ONE STOP AWAY FROM A SHIFT

Many of us assume that leading a happy life means avoiding negative emotions, like stress, sadness, and anger, whenever we can. But instead of suppressing those unpleasant emotions, what if we could find power in them to improve our lives? Caring for your mental well-being is the answer. You're not trapped in your current behavior patterns or thought patterns. Once you become aware of them and notice them, you have the capacity to change. *Stop & Shift* is a transformational mental skill that has the power to open minds and change hearts, and I couldn't be more excited to share it with you here.

Stop stands for:

Silence
Thoughts
On
Purpose

This is where you develop mature self-awareness and strengthen your ability to identify negative or harmful thoughts, quiet the noise, and check in with yourself.

Just to be clear, in this first step, *Stop*, I am not telling you to ignore or run from any uncomfortable emotions or thoughts. Suppressing discomfort only delays your growth, and eventually those things you're trying to bury deep down will come to the surface and manifest in unhealthy behaviors. *Stop* is the pause that allows you to become more aware of your thoughts instead of letting them take you on an emotional roller coaster. When you notice the thought, then you're no longer trapped in it. That's a superpower.

We'll unpack this more in later chapters.

Being able to stop negative thoughts from spiraling isn't enough, though; we then need to point them in a healthy direction. That's why we ***Shift***. Shifting helps create a mindset that's:

Strong
Healthy
Intentional
Focused
Transformed

Shifting your focus is absolutely critical to taking your power back because what you focus on becomes your life. Immeasurable blessings are all around you when you stay open, which is why it's important to shift yourself to a positive, open state when you notice you're stuck in a sour or closed space.

My soul work is to give beautiful humans, like you, techniques and mental skills that will help you live a rich, full, authentic life. I'm doing my part, but you have to do the work too. It's going to take some practice, you're going to have to commit to doing reps and hitting those mental burpees, but I assure you, friend, when you adjust your perspective and commit to positive thinking, you're in store for a mindshift that will radically change your life.

CHILL OUT

In today's world, we're overstimulated, and our attention is constantly pulled in various directions. For that reason (and plenty more), we need to rewire our brains by enforcing quiet time.

When you feel stuck on an idea or your brain just feels cloudy, the best thing you can do is give it the space it needs to relax, wander, and flow. We tend to feel uneasy when we're not moving, doing, or talking. But there's power in being still and silent… Lying on the floor in total silence is one of the most spiritually and mentally replenishing things you can do for yourself. Let your whole self rest and rejuvenate for five to ten minutes.

Rules to chill:

- Put your phone in a different room (if you're using it as a timer, you can set it outside of the room so it's not a distraction but close enough for you to hear the alarm).
- Lie on the floor.
- Breathe.
- Let the thoughts flow without feeling attached to them. When you focus on one thought, you limit your ability to observe other ideas.
- If you need to, keep a pad of paper and pen (not your phone or other electronic device) nearby for any thoughts. Don't write down full phrases, as that will eat up your "still time." Just drop key words on the paper so you can go back and review in more depth later. The point of this exercise is not to spend time writing but to create mental space for many ideas to flow.

> *"Every morning when you wake up, new baby nerve cells have been born while you are sleeping that are there at your disposal to be used in tearing down toxic thoughts and rebuilding healthy thoughts."*
>
> —Dr. Caroline Leaf

3

Yes, This Will Work for You

Your brain doesn't control your thinking; your thinking controls your brain.

Say whaaat??

Yep, it's true. Sometimes we get so consumed by our nonstop, fast 'n furious thoughts that it's hard to disconnect from the noise. And when we get that deep into our own internal narratives, it's easy to lose sight of the fact that *our brain* and *our thoughts* are really separate things.

I'm gonna let you sit with that one for a minute.

Okay, you back with me? This is so important, I think it's worth saying again. Your *brain* and your *thoughts* are separate things. YES! Your brain may create thoughts, but your brain is not those thoughts. And you actually have a built-in tool that helps you shape your brain and recognize your thoughts—your mind.

That's right, I'm telling you that your brain, your thoughts, and your mind are all separate! They're so tightly integrated that it can be hard to see the distinctions at first, but the more you start noticing your thoughts and strengthening your mind, the more you will become attuned to this.

Now, here's the beautiful thing about those three pieces being separate yet connected: even though you can't block unwanted thoughts from randomly popping up in your head, you can learn how to use your mind to create space from them. That's going to let you observe them objectively, which ultimately shapes your brain.

In the midst of my deepest pain, I had no clue the power I possessed simply in *choosing* my thoughts. I definitely didn't think I could control my mind, because I felt like my mind was driving me crazy! It was so hard to find words to explain the broad range of sporadic thoughts that were constantly running through my head, and even harder to make sense of it all. That's because I was wrestling with them instead of making room to process them. I was completely engrossed. I was all up on those thoughts like white on rice before I figured out how to use my mind to create some space.

When I would envision my husband in the gym, my body would respond. I'd feel sick, get an intense headache, and experience physical pain that didn't make sense. Then I would get mad that I felt bad, and this started the downward spiral. I eventually figured out that the only way I could break out of the negative cycle and move past these physical side effects was by allowing the emotions to flow through me and then managing my thoughts.

Sounds backwards, doesn't it? I know. The natural response to upsetting emotions would be to run the opposite direction and dodge them at all costs! But intuitively, I knew that I couldn't run forever and would eventually have to deal with the pain. So instead of avoiding it, I faced it head on. Let me show you what I mean by describing one of my meltdowns.

It was a few months after Rich died. I was in my house, feeling lost and completely alone. Everything in my life was being ripped apart and destroyed, and I felt like I was drowning. I remember being in the kitchen, thinking about how my husband would often kiss me on my forehead and say, "I love you," just because. That thought triggered the waterworks.

I walked into the living room and sat on the couch, tucked my knees up to my chin, and just sobbed. Sitting there, I started thinking about our evening ritual of watching old reruns. I remembered one night in particular: Rich was sitting there killing a carton of Ben & Jerry's Cherry Garcia ice cream when he said, "Do you think my clients would believe that I eat like this? Would they be mad that I don't follow a strict diet?" I started laughing until my cheeks hurt because as he pondered these questions out loud, he never took his eyes off the ice cream. He looked at it longingly, knowing good and well he didn't care what his clients thought—nothing could get between him and his Cherry Garcia.

That memory led to other memories, and the tears continued to flow, heavier and faster. My mind was bouncing all over the place from loving thoughts to angry ones and then enraged emotions. Before I knew it, I was completely consumed.

My head started pounding. I rolled from the couch onto the floor, and by this point, my entire body was overcome with pain. I laid down on the ground and sobbed. I yelled out, asking the big question: *WHY?* Why did Rich have to die? Why did he have to die like *that*? Why was my life falling apart? Why was everything being stripped away?

With my heart shattered into a million little pieces on the floor, the more I talked out loud, the more my jaw and throat felt strained. Finally, I stopped talking and just cried until I couldn't cry anymore. By the time the tears dried, I noticed something, I felt physically lighter. This helped my mind open up a bit, and that's when I surrendered and prayed:

God, if I've learned anything, it's that life is out of our control. No one can control what's around the corner; even the most organized, skilled planner will never fully know what the future holds. Life is just…unpredictable. So, I surrender. I don't know the reason all of this is happening, and I may never know, but I'm not going to overthink it. I can't; it's draining me. I'm just going to do my best and take it one breath at a time. One breath at a time, one breath at a time.

That prayer stuck with me, because when other difficult moments followed (for years to come), I would remind myself, *Take it one breath at a time.*

I don't know where I first heard this quote, but it has become the foundation of my encouragement to the broken-hearted: "You can be mad, sad, angry, disappointed, frustrated; you can go to crazy town if you need to—just don't build your house there!" That's the messy part of healing and growth. On this journey, you have to be willing to face the ugly parts, flow with them, and learn from them so they don't get bottled up inside.

Little did I know, I was practicing mindfulness. Instead of living in the past or being anxious about the future, I would bring myself into the present moment. Of course, I was still sad and hurt; nothing can rush the healing process. But when I noticed my thoughts creating physically adverse symptoms, I would take a beat (sometimes this would include deep breathing, letting tears flow, praying) to let things flow and then intentionally shift my focus to something really specific like, *I'm thankful I have clean water and a roof over my head. I'm grateful for these clean sheets and that my son is healthy…*

I started noticing that changing the thought would change my energy.

This disciplined action was engaging a part of my brain—the prefrontal cortex (remember, the CEO)—that helped lead to other healthy choices. Discipline led to consistency, and consistency led to transformation. That's the power that's inside all of us.

I had no idea all of the benefits that would follow this conscious behavior. It wasn't until later, when I immersed myself in learning about mindfulness, positive psychology, and neuroplasticity, that I discovered managing our thoughts actually

Change your thought—change your energy.

changes the brain chemically, structurally, and functionally. As I learned more from reading other people's research, I started to understand how and why I was able to develop a healthy mindset despite the heinous crime our family suffered. It wasn't like a light-switch moment, a quick sudden change. It was more like a dimmer switch—slowly, as I gathered more evidence, things got brighter and clearer. Through practice, focus, and healthy habits, I'd transformed my thinking, which ultimately transformed my life.

Scrolling through Pinterest one day, a quote jumped off the page and nearly smacked me in the forehead. It read, "You are responsible for your healing." *smack*

That right there is straight up TRUTH. And I'd add to that—we're also responsible for the thoughts we dwell on.

I know it sometimes feels like your brain is driving you bonkers, but when you develop these mental skills, not only will you be able to observe your thoughts; you will also feel empowered to choose whether or not you listen to or engage with them. Keep in mind that whatever you decide has consequences, because what you focus on becomes your life.

Reliving a bad memory over and over again. Focusing on negative emotions. Stewing over a conversation that rubbed you the wrong way. That kind of negative thinking will produce damaging consequences, like adding more stress to your brain and body. On the flip side, positive thinking also has consequences—the good kind. Concentrating on uplifting thoughts not only feels good; it enhances the brain structure and its functionality by creating new neural connections. Remember, neurons that fire together wire together.

I don't know about you, but knowing that I can choose my thoughts, and that my thoughts rewire my brain, makes it easier for me to decide what to focus on. I want the good stuff, and I bet you do too. In this world where negativity is ridiculously loud—it's literally everywhere we turn—we need to make a stronger effort to magnify the positive. Be intentional about amplifying the good!

To be clear, I am not about to preach toxic positivity. Nope, not for a second. That kind of mindset dismisses real emotions by encouraging you just to "carry on." We cannot—I repeat, *cannot*—suppress our troubles; that does more harm than good in the long run. So instead of stuffing it down, imagine being able to face adversity or rejection or stress, and rather than coming away feeling broken, you emerge feeling stronger. Our brain is a sophisticated muscle, and our mind is a superpower tool, but like many things in life, they did not come with an owner's guide when we were born. Thankfully, we live in a time where scientists and researchers are learning more and more about how we can use this tool (the mind) to strengthen this muscle (the brain) and not only build our resilience to get through the hard stuff, but more importantly, unlock limitless joy, unwavering peace, deep gratitude, and so much more.

Be intentional about amplifying the good!

In the next few pages, I'm going to share my CliffsNotes from the last few years of studying the human mind. Specifically, I'm going to walk you through the three areas that helped me better understand why *Stop & Shift* is so effective: mindfulness, positive psychology, and neuroplasticity. I seriously wish I could see your face as you dive into the upcoming pages because it is so fun to witness the light-bulb moments when I share this info with clients or others in person. Since I can't see your beautiful face at this moment, I'd love it if you would snap a pic of yourself with the book and share your biggest takeaway. Tag me on Instagram (@karen.m.allen) so I can drop by and show some love!

Okay, let's do this...

MINDFULNESS IS MORE THAN MEDITATION

Merriam-Webster defines mindfulness as "the practice of maintaining a nonjudgmental state of heightened or complete awareness of one's thoughts, emotions, or experiences on a moment-to-moment basis."[4]

According to *Wikipedia*, mindfulness is "the psychological process of purposely bringing one's attention to experiences occurring in the present moment without judgment, which one can develop through the practice of meditation and through other training."[5]

I think a blended, condensed version of the two could be: *the practice of maintaining a calm and focused mind.*

What I particularly appreciate about the *Wikipedia* definition is that last portion of the sentence: "which one can develop through the practice of meditation *and through other training.*"

This is important to note because people often think mindfulness and meditation are synonymous. Really, meditation is one of many mindfulness exercises, but it's not the only way to practice and develop mindfulness. Think back to the parallel between mental strength training and physical strength training. We know there are so many different exercises we can do, and should do, to develop our overall physical strength, right? Yoga, lifting weights, resistance training, Pilates, dancing—these are all variations of physical activity that help you get stronger and build your endurance.

Think of mindfulness like a mental workout. There are different exercises you can do to add up to a great workout: meditation, deep breathing, journaling, reading, resting, and walking, just to name a few. Every time you do one of these exercises, you're developing a stronger, healthier, more resilient mindset. You are quite literally training your mind and nourishing your brain.

The key to mindfulness is practicing being fully present in the moment, which strengthens your awareness, focus, and attention. Meditation is a popular mindfulness exercise because you practice being present by focusing your attention on your breath, but mindfulness is so much more than that. The very essence of mindfulness is being mindful, and there are a ton of activities that can strengthen this muscle, which will help you focus, slow down, and even de-stress.

> I've included a special gift at the end of this chapter—51 Mental Strength Training Exercises. There are so many simple activities that you can do (mindfully) to care for your mental health.

For example, walking is one of the best forms of exercise, but it packs double the value when you make it a mindfulness exercise by bringing yourself into the moment instead of letting your mind race with worries, deadlines, or grocery lists. Instead, be aware of your surroundings. Notice the leaves, listen to the sounds around you, take a few deep breaths and let the fresh air fill your lungs. And when your thoughts do start to wander, as they will, use your senses to gently bring your attention back to the moment you're in. No need to get frustrated if your mind wanders a lot; mine does too—we're human. Plus, bringing your thoughts back to the present moment is good practice, and *practice makes progress.*

In *Stop & Shift, Stop* is the mindful moment, the pause, that gives you space to consider your options, problem-solve, and maintain composure before acting in a way you might later regret. Irrational behavior is purely a result of internal chaos, which is why the pause is so powerful—it gives you a beat to become aware of what's bubbling up inside of you and what's going on around you.

The more you practice mindfulness in your day-to-day life, the easier it is to *Stop* when you're about to flip out on your kid, or give the inconsiderate vendor a piece of your mind, or scream at a random driver on the interstate. Making a daily practice of doing mindful reps builds your strength for the tough moments when you really need to take a beat and consider your response to the situation. Some reactions are justified, but what we want to practice is choosing a response that is most helpful to the situation. I once heard someone say, "Choosing how you react is the single most powerful, courageous, badass thing a human can do." I agree.

YOU WERE CREATED TO FLOURISH

Several years ago, I stumbled on a YouTube video of a handful of professors answering the question: "What is positive psychology?" I'll never forget one of their responses: "Positive psychology is a shift in one of humankind's biggest questions, 'What's wrong with us?' to 'What's right with us?'"[6] I heard this again and again over the years in different articles and online courses. What they mean is, traditional psychology looks at things that are "wrong," or our brokenness—things like anxiety, depression, or trauma. Positive psychology looks at what's *right,* or our strengths—things like resilience, purpose, courage, grit, flow, and our ability to adapt and evolve. It looks at the best of the human condition, how we function optimally. Another one of the definitions that came from that video was "the study of how humans flourish." That's my fave.

I was beyond thrilled to discover that we're not just born with a limited amount of resilience and our joy doesn't tap out at a certain point. No, friend, you can learn specific strategies that will help you strengthen these amazing qualities with practice. As I dove in deeper to my studies, it hit me—*Stop & Shift* is one of those strategies! It helps us shift ourselves into a positive state by leveraging positive traits.

But this is more than looking at the bright side; it's choosing how you want to live. It's about building a life of meaning. One of the most insightful TikToks I've ever shared was of a man who put this in perspective for all of us. He said, "Imagine if you wake up every day with $84,600 in your bank account, and every day, at the end of the night, it's gone, whether you used it or not. And then the next day you get another $84,600. You would do everything in your power to spend it, because you know the next day you're getting $84,600. You don't wanna leave nothin' there. You want to make the best of it, right? You get 84,600 seconds. Why waste time? It doesn't carry over."[7] Let that sink in.

> Stop & Shift helps us shift ourselves into a positive state by leveraging positive traits.

Those 84,600 seconds per day are ours to use however we want, so let's not waste them being negative. Take every moment and be intentional, because time is precious—it doesn't roll over to the next day.

Part of being 100% human is accepting that we can't control the thoughts coming into our mind—but we can decide how long they stay. Busy thoughts can be our biggest downfall if we don't learn how to manage them. Mindfulness will help strengthen your attention, which helps you notice when you're stuck in a negative thought cycle—that's the *Stop*. Then, in swoops the power of positive psychology, which helps you reverse the flow of your thoughts from a negative downward spiral to a positive upward spiral—that's the *Shift*. Learning how to shift your thoughts might seem like a small adjustment, but don't underestimate the power of little changes, friend. They go a long way. As the saying goes, "Small hinges move big doors."

In a *Forbes* article on the work of Scott Glassman, founder of A Happier You, Rob Dupe writes, "Deciding to change your whole mindset from negative to positive sounds like an overwhelming challenge.... Instead of treating this journey as one big task, break it down into smaller steps." According to Glassman, "It makes the change so much more manageable,"[8]

Each positive or productive shift is a small step. A small, but mighty, step forward.

BRAIN GAINS

Remember when I told you that when neurons fire together, they wire together? This action leads to new neural connections in our brains, which is what I like to call *brain gains*. As neurons fire together again and again over time, these new neural connections lead to a "rewiring" of the brain. Every time you stop a negative thought cycle and shift to a more positive narrative, you're developing new neural connections. Neuroplasticity is the ability of the brain to form new connections and pathways and change how its circuits are wired, which in essence means that regardless of what has happened to you up until this point, you have the ability to make small changes that over time will produce life-changing results.

One book that helped me better understand how complex and advanced our brains are is *Switch On Your Brain* by Dr. Caroline Leaf. It's absolutely fascinating to learn how powerful our mind is—so powerful, it can quite literally change the structure of our brain.

> "Your brain will follow the instructions and choices of your mind and change its landscape accordingly."
>
> "Whether we switch on happiness, peace, and good health or switch on anxiety, worry, and negativity, we are changing the physical substance of the brain."
>
> —Dr. Caroline Leaf, *Switch On Your Brain*[9]

Have you ever heard someone say, "Think positive thoughts"? You may have brushed past that advice, but it's actually a powerful mental exercise. Beliefs, dreams, hopes, and thoughts make a tremendous impact on how the brain functions. We should practice thinking positive thoughts because it boosts our brilliance, while, on the flip side, toxic thinking wears down the brain.

> "As you think those negative thoughts about the future—the week ahead, what a person might say or do, even in the absence of the concrete stimulus— that toxic thinking will change your brain wiring in a negative direction and throw your mind and body into stress."
>
> —Dr. Caroline Leaf, *Switch On Your Brain*[10]

A footnote to the quote above reveals that "98% of mental and physical illness comes from our thought life."[11] But I didn't need a book to tell me that; I've felt it. I've had moments where my frantic thoughts have made me feel like I was going to either pass out or be sick to my stomach. Now it just makes more sense why that happens, and honestly, it makes me feel more hopeful because we hold the power and have the free will to choose how we focus our attention, which directly affects the chemicals and, subsequently, the wiring of our brain. The choices we make create real, legitimate consequences, not just in life but also in our brain.

I wish more people knew how powerful their minds really were. But you get it; that's why you're here. You realize that something needs to change, and whatever "it" is, it starts with your thoughts and your mindset. *Stop & Shift* is just one of many tools that can help you rewire your brain. Just like an athlete develops their physical strength by training every day, the more you practice this tool, the more skilled you'll become and the stronger your brain will be. It's time to start taking better care of our thoughts and our minds instead of leaving our brains unprotected from the chaos of this world.

The choice is yours—choose wisely!

> "Today our culture is undergoing an epidemic of toxic thoughts that, left unchecked, create ideal conditions for illnesses."
>
> —Dr. Caroline Leaf, *Switch On Your Brain*[12]

META-WHAAT?

Metacognition is a fancy word for *thinking about your thoughts*. It's what happens when you analyze what's going on, plan an approach, take action, and then reflect and adjust your approach. This can happen rapidly or over a long stretch of time. And in some cases, it can be so automatic that it can seem invisible.

Stop & Shift is a metacognition technique because it helps you reflect on and improve your mindset and move to higher, more masterful levels of thinking and living. It teaches you how to analyze what you're doing and how you're thinking so you can adjust your actions to meet your goals in life.

For example, my goal when I first started applying mindfulness techniques was healing. I wanted to feel happy, healthy, and whole, so I would reflect on different areas of life—my thought cycles, people, situations, work—and analyze if they were bringing me closer to or further away from my goal, and adjust as necessary.

Your thought processes will become more sophisticated the more you practice metacognition, and your mind will become more adept at analyzing your thoughts to choose the best response.

Here's an example of how fast this can happen. (For all my fellow parents out there who want to be more patient, please feel encouraged that you don't have to be perfect; you just have to practice showing up in a mindful way.)

One morning as my son, Caleb, was getting ready for school, I was multitasking doing household chores like moving the laundry from the washer to the dryer, making beds, and packing his snack for the day. I asked him to brush his teeth, so we could make our way out the door, and continued on to the next task that needed my attention.

When I walked by the bathroom, I noticed he had his toothbrush in hand but he was NOT brushing his teeth. Instead, he was using it to sword fight the water as it flowed from the faucet.

"Caleb, focus, man," I said gently as I walked by.

On my way back from the bedroom, again I noticed he was still in his own little imaginary world. "Caleb, c'mon, dude; we need to get out of the door," I said, this time a little agitated.

Finally, after I finished getting my shoes on, I walked into the bathroom and he was still sword fighting the water.

"CALEB! I told you we need to go. Why are you still playing! We're going to be late, and I have a lot to do today. GET IT TOGETHER!!!" I screamed…in my head.

That's right, I noticed these thoughts firing off in my mind and was able to catch them before they ripped through my little guy's joyful spirit. When I heard the fury, I paused and asked myself, "Karen, do you really want to start his day like this? Your anger will be the voice he hears in his head. Not to mention, he's just being a kid, so ease up."

The time it took to shift from an angry reaction to a reasonable response was a matter of seconds. Why? Because I've trained my brain to think before I speak, to pause and process, so I can consciously choose the best response instead of an emotionally charged one. And you can, too.

Instead of unleashing the fury of my frustration, I took a beat, walked into the bathroom, got down to his eye level, and said, "Caleb, I know you're having fun. Playing with water feels so good! But right now I need you to brush your teeth so we can get to school. When you get home, we can definitely have some water play. Sound good?"

And just like that, with a *Stop* and a *Shift*, instead of my son's day starting with anger, he left the house happy and looking forward to our water play plans after school.

THE OPTIMAL MINDSET

Dr. Carol Dweck, a Stanford University research psychologist and author of one of my favorite books, *Mindset*, completely rocked my world with the term "growth mindset." Even if you've heard this term before, let's just take a few moments to unpack it because, well, it IS the end goal here. First, what is a growth mindset…

> "[The] *growth mindset* is based on the belief that your basic qualities are things you can cultivate through your efforts…everyone can change and grow through application and experience."
>
> —Dr. Carol Dweck, *Mindset*[13]

In short, *effort and experience help you change and grow*. But not only that— check this out. This was one of the first highlighted passages in the book that made my jaw drop:

> "The passion for stretching yourself and sticking to it, even (or especially) when it's not going well, is the hallmark of a growth mindset. *This is the mindset that allows people to thrive during some of the most challenging times in their lives."*
>
> —Dr. Carol Dweck, *Mindset*[14]

This says it all, folks—right here in black and white. Your mindset is what can and *will* get you to the other side of life's storms and tough moments.

Now don't get it twisted—this doesn't mean it'll be easy or pain free. Even with a growth mindset, adversity doesn't feel "good." People with a growth mindset still feel pain, but instead of letting it fester or spiral out of control, we simply see it as a problem to face, manage, and grow from. We brave difficulties with perseverance, a toolbox of strategies, and a focus on learning. We use hardships and setbacks as launching pads for growth.

The moment I realized I had a choice—that I could either sit in my misery or do something productive with it—was a big shift moment. Instead of letting this experience destroy me, I wanted to use it to become a better person.

Although much of Dweck's work is focused on students developing their learning capacity, she also mentioned in her studies that "the *more* depressed people with the growth mindset felt (short of severe depression), the *more* they took action to confront their problems…. The worse they felt, the more determined they became" to overcome the negativity and push through to the other side.[15]

The deeper I dove into growth mindset studies, the more I saw this mindset as the pathway to optimal living. If you want to live a joyful, successful, peaceful life, it's possible only with a growth mindset. Why? Because life can be unfair—it's not easy, and it's definitely not predictable—but a growth mindset will help you approach challenging moments with both resilience and flexibility.

Bottom line? You can develop a growth mindset with effort and application. The more mental exercises you practice, the stronger your mind will become. *Stop & Shift* will help you develop a growth mindset and, eventually, transform your way of thinking.

Let's not waste any more time…here we go.

51 Mental Strength Training Exercises

1. Spend time with empowering people.
2. Avoid multitasking.
3. Drink lots of water.
4. Distance yourself from things that don't feel good.
5. Take breaks from social media and your phone.
6. Identify the small things that make you excited.
7. Smile on purpose as much as possible.
8. Practice deep breathing.
9. Color mindfully.
10. Face one of your fears.
11. Journal.
12. Listen to music.
13. Talk to someone.
14. Watch motivational videos on YouTube.
15. Take a day off work.
16. Make lists of things you want to do.
17. Eat extra fruits and veggies.
18. Meditate.
19. Read.
20. Treat yourself in whatever way makes sense.
21. Look for opportunities to show random acts of kindness.
22. Regularly reflect on lessons you learn.
23. Write a list of compliments to yourself.
24. Do yoga.
25. Mind map a major goal.
26. Forgive others, and yourself.
27. Make a gratitude list.
28. Take a walk in nature.
29. Take a relaxing shower.
30. Declutter your space.

31. Sing and dance like nobody's watching.
32. Observe your thoughts; let them come and go freely.
33. Exercise or get some movement on a regular basis.
34. Create work hour boundaries.
35. Leave toxic and negative relationships.
36. Ask for help.
37. Give yourself a pep talk.
38. Do something new and creative.
39. Clean out your closet and donate to a local charity.
40. Garden—get your hands dirty.
41. Avoid social comparisons.
42. Get enough sleep and adequate rest.
43. Make a playlist of feel-good songs.
44. Identify things that deplete your energy and try to remove them.
45. Reflect on what your ideal day looks like.
46. Eat all of your meals phone free.
47. Check in periodically: *How do I feel at the moment?*
48. Work on releasing things that are out of your control.
49. Don't force anything.
50. Use chore time as an opportunity to observe your thoughts.
51. Tune in to your intuition.

PART

STOP

" You have the ability to free yourself. Whether you choose to do so or not is entirely up to you. "

4

The Voice Inside Your Head

Stop is all about the inner voice.

Everyone has a *voice* inside their head. Maybe yours just said, *I don't have a voice in my head.* Yep, that's the one. Don't worry—before you panic and think you're crazy—it's normal, I promise. I'll paint a quick picture that will hopefully put your heart at ease and help you realize just how normal this is:

You jump in your car. Turn on the ignition. Put it in drive and head out to your destination. And then, after driving for a bit, you suddenly recognize you're heading in the wrong direction. You were so lost in your thoughts that you didn't realize where you were going. Physically, you were in the car, but mentally, you were living in another world.

Sound familiar? Everyone's done that at least once in their lifetime.

It's kind of impressive that your mind can create a separate reality from the one you're presently living. But when you're not aware of it, it can also be dangerous and can result in unconscious behavior, uncalculated responses, and in the long run, unintended outcomes.

There are many, many examples of this:

➤ You might be walking through the grocery store, but in your head, you're replaying an argument with your significant other.

➤ You're at work in front of the computer, typing away, but your mind is bouncing around different thoughts, like worrying about the kids, repeating a coworker's snide comment, reflecting on your best friend's infertility news, or feeling consumed by all of the what-ifs triggered by the overwhelm of negative news.

The mind is always busy. It can build a world of fear, chaos, and havoc, even if you're just sitting at the breakfast table, eating a bowl of cereal. The wild thing is, not only do we create an alternate universe, but someone else is the tour guide! That's right—that pesky little voice inside your head, the one that won't turn off. It's there when you drive, when you're in the shower, when you're trying to fall asleep—so annoying.

A 2005 study by the National Science Foundation revealed that we think anywhere between 12,000 and 60,000 thoughts a day.[16] *Per day*, my friend! That's a lot of thinking, energy, and nonstop chatter. And when you start to notice it, you'll see your thoughts bounce around, without rhyme or reason, like three-year-olds on an intense sugar rush. When your brain is in this state, it's often referred to as "the monkey mind," because it is jumping all over the place. Our thoughts become so sporadic—they could be of a plan, a person, a future goal, a memory, a feeling, anything!

Thoughts of the past...
I wish I'd started that workout routine last month.
When she said that, did she really mean _____?
I can't believe I forgot to return those shoes again.
I think my fourth-grade teacher's name was Mrs. Greene.

Thoughts of the future...
I'm going to eat healthy next week. Note to self: check Pinterest later for "clean meal" ideas.
If I take the subway, then I could get there 15 minutes faster.
What if I take that director role and hate it?
We should go to San Francisco in the fall...I wonder if Shelly will be in town.

Your to-do list...
Call the pediatrician to schedule the kid's next wellness appointment.
Send Rob that email to give him these price quotes.
Did I put the laundry in the dryer?
Pick up batteries on the way home.

Your inner critic...
Do you really think you should apply for that promotion? It hasn't even been a year.
No one's going to read my blog.
Why even start a new workout? It's not like I have a strong track record of sticking to a routine.
Get real, you have too much baggage for someone to want to date you.

When I started practicing *Stop & Shift*, I realized I was wasting too much time and mental energy on things that were out of my control. I was chasing every "what-if," or carrying someone else's baggage that was not mine to carry, or feeling heavy with all of my worries and anxiety. Winston Churchill said, "When I look back on all these worries, I remember the story of the old man who said on his deathbed that he had had a lot of trouble in his life, most of which had never happened."[17] A study published by Lucas S. LaFreniere and Michelle G. Newman confirms this anecdote, revealing that 80–90% of the worries that we dwell on don't even happen.[18] I know I can definitely relate to this factoid. Can you?

The goal of this first step is to notice the voice so you create a break in your stream of thoughts. You literally need to interrupt your thoughts, because if you don't, that nagging voice can be a distraction, or even worse—destructive to your mental health. In this chapter, we're going to build your awareness of this voice so you can look at your thoughts objectively, create space from unwanted emotions in a healthy way that allows them to flow, and quiet the inner critic so you can hear your intuition more clearly. Tuning in to the voice gives you the room to choose which thoughts you're going to lean into and which ones you need to release.

> Tuning in to your inner voice gives you the room to choose which thoughts you're going to lean into and which ones you need to release.

YOU ARE NOT YOUR THOUGHTS

The voice that's narrating your thoughts is separate from you. Once you're aware of it, you begin the process of creating some space so it will no longer control you. The more you develop and strengthen your awareness, the easier it is to notice the voice without being absorbed by it.

Michael Singer, the author of *The Untethered Soul*, helps us single out the voice in a very simple exercise:

> *You are the one who hears the voice. You are the one who notices that it's talking.*
> *You do hear it when it talks, don't you? Make it say "hello" right now. Say it over and over a few times. Now shout it inside! Can you hear yourself saying "hello" inside? Of course you can.*[19]

In psychological lingo, the voice you hear inside your head is called "inner speech." We use it every day—for example, when going through shopping lists or motivating ourselves to get up and exercise. And unless you're a speed reader who's trained their brain not to use the voice while reading, chances are you're probably using it right now while reading this sentence.

Singer's exercise is a great way to help you practice seeing your inner dialogue objectively. The same way you can look across the room and see a table, or look outside and see a tree, we should also look at our thoughts as objects of our attention. Thoughts are just a focal point in the mind, a focal point that changes with the wind. Seeing them as separate from you, instead of attaching yourself to every single one, helps create the space you need to protect your inner peace, think clearly in a heated moment, and be more intentional about where you're directing your attention.

Imagine, for a moment, being angry at your child for not following your directions for the eighteenth time, but instead of screaming your head off—and then feeling guilty about it later—you catch your words before they launch out of your mouth. You notice the anger boiling up, you feel the words that you want to yell forming in your head, but instead of leaning into that negative energy, you take a pause.

And in that pause, you visualize your options—you see two paths. The first path is an emotionally charged outburst that ends in your child crying, feeling hurt, and becoming closed off to anything you have to say. The second path is a more composed approach that includes you sharing your frustrations in an honest, healthy way and coming up with a solution with your child to help them follow the directions you've had to repeat several times. Both options are just thoughts, imagery in your mind; neither is YOU until you decide to participate in it.

Let's do a quick exercise to help you notice your thoughts objectively. Here's what it looked like when I sat for a few minutes and tuned in to that voice in my head:

I hate going to the gym, but I could work out at home.

I like this song.

It's so breezy out, I should sit outside.

My back hurts. I need to work out.

Did I send that email?

What's for dinner?

I gotta remember to text Taryn!

Maybe we should go to Chipotle tonight, I don't feel like cooking.

I'm going to set up that email series before the end of the week.

I think I have cheese here, I could make queso. Or, I could make mac n cheese.

Now it's your turn. Take out a piece of paper and sit quietly for two to three minutes. During that silence, jot down any thoughts that pop into your head. Go ahead, I'll be here when you get back…

The same way you can see those thoughts on paper, you can look at them in your mind—it just takes practice. I once heard someone describe the process of noticing your thoughts like sitting on the bank of a river watching sticks and logs float by in the water. Those sticks and logs are your thoughts. You can choose to pick them up, play with them, stare at them, and keep them, or you can let 'em float on by. The choice is yours, but *first*, you have to pay attention to what's going on in your mind. It takes awareness to build awareness.

Cognitive defusion is a fancy term for *looking **at** your thoughts rather than **from** them*. Originally called *cognitive distancing* by the founder of cognitive therapy, Dr. Aaron Beck, it's a process where we detach from our stream of thoughts so we can choose how we engage with them. This technique helps you strengthen your mindset to respond to your thoughts with conscious action instead of an automatic, emotionally charged reaction. It's about stepping back from your thoughts so that you're able to see them as separate from you—something you can notice and release rather than something that necessarily overtakes your mind and life. When you practice observing your internal dialogue, it will supercharge your self-awareness.

This is the beginning of your mindset reset. Recognize your inner speech. *Stop*. Take a pause to look at your thoughts and break the negative thought cycle. Notice the voice so you can begin to catch the thoughts that are draining, unhelpful, and pointless. Your thoughts shouldn't have so much power over you. You are not your thoughts! They are simply in your head until they come out in the form of words or actions—and *how* they come out is always under your control.

Okay, now that we're able to notice the voice, let's talk about how to create some mental space from it.

MR. TURTLE AND MR. FOX

I heard a wise Buddhist parable called "Mr. Turtle and Mr. Fox" that offers a great illustration of how we should engage with our thoughts. It goes something like this:

One day, Mr. Turtle was making his way down a path toward the lake. Mr. Fox was off in the distance walking on the same path toward Mr. Turtle. When Mr. Turtle saw this danger up ahead, he thought to himself, "What should I do? I'm not fast enough to run."

He realized his only protection was his shell. When Mr. Fox got closer, Mr. Turtle went into his shell. Mr. Fox started hovering around, and meanwhile, Mr. Turtle was thinking, "Let me remain in my shell with a calm mind and much patience."

Eventually, Mr. Fox got tired of hovering around and gave up the mission and went away.

In life, we face many foxes, such as stress, worries, tension, pain, anxiety, fear, sadness…the list goes on. When we encounter these foxes, we should be like Mr. Turtle. And this doesn't mean what you're probably thinking—the story isn't saying we should hide or run from our problems. It's suggesting that we observe them instead of wrestling with them. These foxy feelings are passing thoughts, and you can control how you engage with them.

Want to know my go-to move when I need to find some space in my head? You're never going to believe this because it's going to seem too simple, but then when you try it, it might feel too hard… This is what I do. Brace yourself. Ready?? I lay down, close my eyes, and watch my thoughts like a show—like I'm flipping through channels on the TV. If you think of your mind like a television and your thoughts are the shows, then when you don't like what you see, you can just change the channel by *Shifting* your attention. And sometimes, when I'm overreacting about some ridiculous worst-case scenario, I'll eventually laugh out loud to myself because when I pause and play it out in my head, I can see how I'm catastrophizing the situation. You know, sometimes it's good just to run through the absolute worst-case scenario in your head to notice how far-fetched it is. This can actually help you balance out that emotion with logic.

Every thought that comes up isn't meant to be chased. Some are just passing through like the sticks and logs in a river. When you give your thoughts space, you can let them flow through you. Jeff Warren, a writer and meditator, helped me better understand the concept of creating space to cultivate mental calmness. He's such an amazing guide! Jeff taught me the word *equanimity*—it's like this inner smoothness or composure. His guided meditations help you strengthen this muscle so you can learn to stay open and let the disruptive moments pass by. It's life-changing!

Stop & Shift will also help you build this muscle.

Always keep in mind that it's normal to feel anxious or worried or stressed. That's part of being human! Next time when you notice any foxy feelings stirring up inside, be still, little turtle. Give them space to pass by. And if you feel the urge to yell at the voice, demanding that it chill out, let me just warn you, it doesn't work, friend. That will only cause more tension and stress in your head. You might as well be jumping into a boxing ring with Mr. Fox ready to rumble.

Once you're able to separate yourself from your thoughts, you can boost your mental dexterity by learning how to befriend the voice and use it to your advantage. I know you may be thinking, *Karen, that sounds crazy*. But just trust me on this…

PROBLEM-SOLVING PARTNER

As I mentioned earlier, the voice in your head is completely normal, and you shouldn't see it as a bad thing; in fact, it can be very useful. I know it may feel like it's driving you crazy—been there—but it can actually serve as a *problem-solving partner*. Plus, your intuition is buried beneath the noise, and as you learn how to separate your inner critic from your inner guide, it will become easier to make decisions confidently that are best for your happiness, your well-being, and your success.

> Your intuition is buried beneath the noise. Learn how to separate your inner critic from your inner guide.

The more you pay attention to what's bouncing around in your head, the more power you have to select and disconnect from your thoughts, which makes your mind an ideal space for you to consider various options, or perhaps even consequences, and then choose an appropriate response to any given situation. When you get in tune with your inner voice, you can be in the midst of chaos and confusion but still *choose* to hold on to your inner peace. Those external factors will remain outside of you when you learn to sort through the noise and choose where you focus your attention. The more you practice managing your thoughts, the more you will experience inner peace, power, freedom, and sophisticated problem-solving skills.

Firefighters are a great example of this. They're under a lot of pressure when they respond to a call, and they have to make quick decisions when flames are blazing in front of them. Soldiers as well—in their line of work, mental clarity is critical to making decisions with good judgment in the midst of chaos. Like firefighters and soldiers, you can go inward to do a little risk management before jumping in headfirst, emotions blazing. This could save you a lot of pain and heartache on the back end because you decided to play through the scenario in your mind before reacting carelessly.

That's why we shouldn't try to suppress this voice. Not at all. This inner dialogue is the perfect partner to brainstorm, assess what's going on, and take the time needed to make conscious decisions—in other words, to choose wisely.

Problem-solving is a champion skill. Before you fly off the handle or quit your job or cut someone off on the road, you can literally envision your choice and the possible consequences and talk yourself out of irrational, emotion-based reactions and into a more positive, productive response. This is why awareness is so crucial to the decision-making process. When you don't take a beat to notice the story playing out in your head, the most dominant emotion will surely take hold and manifest in words and actions. But when you give your mind the space it needs to problem-solve, you're back in control and can choose how you want to show up moment to moment.

Speaking of how *you* want to show up, have you ever stopped to imagine your fullest life? I'm not talking about having a lot of money and big houses or many cars. There's nothing wrong with those things, but I'm talking about a full life that makes you feel alive. Part of this mindshift is learning to tune out the noise and tune in to what sets your soul on fire. And maybe you're like I was and you've listened to others so much that you lost yourself along the way. Or you've abandoned yourself because you cared too much about others' opinions.

The thing is, if you want to feel fulfilled, you have to follow your soul, because it knows the way. The beauty of this exercise is that while it helps you manage the negative self-talk and break unhealthy thought cycles, it also helps you rediscover your inner guide. I heard Drew Barrymore lovingly describe her inner guide as Jiminy Cricket. It's the small voice that's there to help us assess risk, find our unique gifts, stay safe, and follow what makes us feel alive. We all have one; we've just got to get quiet enough to hear it.

In order for you to use the *Stop & Shift* technique successfully, it's absolutely imperative that you're able to first notice the voice in your head. If you don't do this, it won't work—period. You have to be aware of it, face those thoughts, and own your choice. Only then will you be able to strengthen your mindset by consciously choosing your response to whatever life brings you.

Yes, there will always be events and circumstances that are out of your control, but it's your comeback—the choices and decisions you make—that shapes your quality of life. Everything in your life—every action and every word—is first a thought. The only way to change the world around you is to first tune in to and notice the world you're creating in your mind.

From here, we *Shift*.

LET THEM RUN WILD

Here's a little exercise to help you practice disconnecting from your thoughts. Grab a pen. Set a timer for three minutes. In the space below (preferably while sitting in silence), write all the thoughts that come to your mind. Literally, anything goes. Ready, set, go!

_____

_____

_____

_____

_____

_____

_____

_____

_____

_____

_____

_____

_____

_____

Wow, friend! Your mind was all over the place. Don't worry, I'm not judging. Shoot, you saw my scattered, all-over-the-place thought pattern just a few pages back.

The thoughts you just wrote on this paper are as independent from you as the thoughts rolling around at a rapid pace in your head. Honestly, most thoughts are fleeting. They come and go pretty quickly. But then there are those that stick around for a while, play over and over again, and tend to stir up trouble. Those are the ones we need to get better at managing.

"AHA!" MOMENT ·

Take a few minutes to think about the information we just covered in chapter 4. Did any light bulbs go off? If so, write them down here. As you learn, new revelations will come to light to help you grow forward. They are important to YOUR unique journey.

_____

_____

_____

_____

_____

_____

_____

_____

_____

_____

_____

_____

_____

_____

_____

_____

_____

_____

_____

_____

_____

_____

_____

_____

> *Choice is the most powerful tool we have. Everything boils down to choice.*

5

The Power of Choice

Shift is all about the choice.

Did you notice in the last chapter that each time I mentioned the voice I also pointed to *choice*? That's because paying attention to that voice and your thoughts is only half the effort needed to transform your mindset. Being aware of the voice in your head and noticing what's bouncing around in your mind is the first step to creating change, but understanding the *power of choice* is equally important. Moment by moment, we are choosing who we want to be.

There's a famous parable about the power of choice. It goes like this:

> *An old Cherokee chief was teaching his grandson about life. "A fight is going on inside me," he said to the boy. "It is a fight between two wolves. One is evil—he is anger, envy, sorrow, regret, greed, arrogance, self-pity, guilt, resentment, inferiority, lies, false pride, superiority, and ego."*

He continued, "The other is good—he is joy, peace, hope, serenity, humility, kindness, benevolence, empathy, generosity, truth, compassion, and loving awareness. The same fight is going on inside you—and inside every other person in the world."

The grandson thought about it for a minute and then asked his grandfather, "Which wolf will win?"

To which the old man simply replied, "The one you feed."

Simply put, where you choose to focus your attention will shape everything in your life. Negativity attracts more negativity, and positivity draws in more positivity.

> Moment by moment, we are choosing who we want to be.

I realized the power of choice when I thought about the person who killed my husband and the fact that he had so many opportunities throughout the day to make a different choice. This moment was heavy and messy. It was a few months after Richard died. I was in the thick of my grief, lying on the floor in a puddle of tears, thinking, *How the hell did I get here?* That's when I started imagining all of the decisions that guy made that led up to that terrible, life-changing moment. I kept thinking about all of the chances he had throughout the day when he could've made a *different* choice:

If only he'd decided not to get in the car.
If only he'd decided not to drive to our gym.
If only he'd turned around at the light.
If only he didn't get out of the car.
If only he'd decided not to walk into the gym.
If only he didn't pull the trigger.

As I envisioned these alternative paths in my mind, it finally hit me like a ton of bricks—*I hold the same power, the power of choice.* Without warning, the question then popped into my mind: *What am I choosing?* I sat with it for a minute. Even though my anger was justified, I could see I was choosing to stew in it. And although being sad was a natural response to losing someone I love, did I really want to be sad forever? Running through these thoughts was almost like watching a storybook playing in my mind. I could see that if I didn't stop giving all of my attention to these unhealthy emotions, they would seep into each moment and poison everything in my life.

Gentle reminder, there's nothing wrong with feeling sad or angry about a situation; those are real emotions—but it is 100% up to you to make a conscious decision not to spread more negativity. When you feel heavy emotions weighing you down, this is the perfect opportunity to practice seeing your thoughts and deciding whether you're going to lean into them or let them flow. Take a beat and create some mental space to see whether they are helpful to the situation or not, even if they are valid.

We all have access to this superpower. You can consciously choose the thoughts, the energy, the actions you want to lean into. You may not be able to predict some events and circumstances in your life, but you can flex your strength by mindfully choosing a positive and productive response. Even when things happen that are completely out of your control, like a spouse's sudden death or losing your job or spilling coffee on your lap before a big meeting, intentionally choosing your response is what makes the most meaningful, long-lasting imprint in your life.

This is powerful, y'all; please don't miss this—what you do and what you *don't* do matter.

What you watch matters.
What you think matters.
What you listen to matters.
What you eat matters.
Whom you surround yourself with matters.

Your entire life is the result of a series of choices. All of your decisions are within your control, point-blank, period. You can actually choose who you're going to be each moment of every day.

Staying in a job you hate—*your decision.*
Being in a toxic relationship—*your decision.*
Ignoring your problems—*your decision.*

Sometimes it's as simple as, "Will I choose to eat McDonald's because it's convenient, or will I choose to make a healthy meal at home because I know it's better for me?" Other times, it's a subconscious reaction that we need to manage so we can choose our response wisely. For example, feeling frustrated and then screaming at the kids or noticing the frustration mounting and then choosing to step away, breathe, and regroup before exploding. The best part is, practicing this disciplined thinking in the little everyday frustrations helps strengthen your mind, and you become better equipped to handle more complex decision-making when the pressure is on.

There are three parts to the *Shift*: acknowledging your starting point, knowing who you want to be, and making intentional choices that align with being that person. The goal isn't to be perfect in every scenario—it's to be more mindful of your choices, knowing that every decision, no matter how big or small, has consequences. When you practice *Stop & Shift*, it's the *Shift* that'll help you retrain your brain to make healthy, conscious choices.

YOUR STARTING POINT

So, what is your starting point?

To answer this, we have to talk about acceptance. At some point in everyone's journey, we all wrestle with acceptance. Let's be real, it's hard to accept some things in life, especially things that are unjust, unfair, or problematic. But when it comes to your growth journey, acceptance plays a significant role in getting you to where you want to be.

Imagine you have plans to go to a friend's housewarming party this weekend. You've never been to their new home so before you leave you open the navigation app on your phone and type in their address. When you do this, the app asks for a starting location, doesn't it? Of course it does, because in order for the map to give you accurate directions to where you're going, it has to know where you're starting. The same goes for your personal growth journey. You have to acknowledge your starting point so you know what direction to take to get to where you want to go.

This was one of the toughest—and also the most freeing—"Aha!" moments of my life, and it came while I was in full-blown pity-party mode. I was sooo angry that I was widowed at only 29 and our future had been ripped away from us. I was enraged and couldn't shake the victim mentality. I was daydreaming that this was all a joke—a terrible, horrible joke that Richard was playing—and he was going to walk into the house at any moment... any moment...anyyyyy...

> You have to acknowledge your starting point to find the correct path.

My heart got heavier, my head cloudier, and my ability to grasp reality was fading with each upsetting thought. Finally, I ran out of what-ifs and surrendered to the hard truth: I had to accept that my husband was gone and there was nothing I could do to bring him back. This made the tears flow even faster as I thought to myself, *But HOW can I accept this? If I accept it, that means it's okay that he's not here and it's okay that he was killed, and I am absolutely NOT okay with any of that.* The thoughts continued to fly: *Damnit, I hate this. Ughhh...I may not be okay with it, but I can't change it; I can't travel back in time.* Somewhere in those sporadic thoughts, I felt a hint of peace flicker when this thought emerged: *Acceptance doesn't have to mean I'm "okay" with this outcome, but I do have to accept where I am today. I have to accept and acknowledge that this is my starting point—and from here, I will build.*

By reading this, you'd think that mindshift came in a matter of moments. It didn't. There were weeks of wrestling with painful thoughts about acceptance before I got to this point. But finally, my heart was ready for the truth. Mature awareness is letting go of what you thought life was supposed to be and embracing where you are now.

Is it easy? No.

Is it necessary? Yes—if you want to take control of the direction of your life.

Accepting my starting point helped me break down some internal barriers that were holding me back. First, it gave me the opportunity to take inventory of the things I needed to let go of so I could take my life forward. For example, I had to let go of the *why, why, why?* thoughts because they were weighing me down and clouding my mind. Second, acceptance helped me release the things that were out of my control so I could spend my energy on healthier actions like taking care of my well-being and my kiddo. An example of this: I had to stop listening to everyone's opinions around Rich's death—their judgment was not mine to carry, and it was also weighing me down. And finally, acceptance helped me take strategic steps in a meaningful direction. Instead of living on autopilot and letting my emotions take the lead, I started making intentional choices that would help me get to where I wanted to be. I was sad, tired, and overwhelmed, and I wanted to feel healthy, happy and whole.

The mindshift is accepting what your life has been up to today. That doesn't mean you're "okay" with what's happened; it means you start here. Maybe you've been laid off, or you just went through a breakup, or you're feeling stuck and unfulfilled—okay, that may be your starting point, but what's going to be your next step? The choice is yours.

YOU ARE WHO YOU CHOOSE TO BE

You choose what you focus on, what you do, what you say. You are *choosing* every single moment of the day. The question is, are you aligning your choices with who you want to be and the life you want to live? If you want a peaceful life, choose peace. If you want to feel happier, choose happiness. If you don't like your job, choose to make a change. You're either choosing to stay the same or you're choosing to take your life in a better direction.

Your choices make a ripple effect; they shape your life and directly impact the lives of those around you. I felt the gravity of making conscious choices deep in my bones when I looked at my son. It was clear to me that my choices inevitably would shape his life. That motivated me to choose wisely and choose with care. And to be honest, the first thing I had to choose was—myself. I couldn't be the mom I wanted to be for Caleb if I didn't make my well-being a priority.

After I accepted that I couldn't change what had happened, I started taking ownership of my response, my effort, and my life moving forward.

If I didn't manage my thinking, I knew I wouldn't have a clear mind to make good decisions. If I didn't get exercise or enough sleep, I knew I wouldn't have the energy to function wholly (and we single parents need ALL the energy we can get). If I didn't protect myself from negativity, I knew I would be inviting in toxic and unhealthy energy. It was time to give my mind a new map. I was determined—*determined* is the exact word I'd say to myself—not to let my son lose both parents.

For you, this transformational journey might start right there, with choosing yourself. If you've been putting your needs on the back burner for too long, I've got you covered; there's a whole chapter on that coming up. But for now, let me just express how critical it is that you *choose you.* Your health, your sanity, your happiness, your safety—YOU are your responsibility.

And don't worry, you're not alone. Most of us need to rewire our thinking around this topic because for so long, we've been programmed to put others' needs above our own, or we follow *someone else's* advice for *our* lives, or we sacrifice what's best for us because we don't want to let others down.

But let me tell you something, friend: it simply doesn't work that way. First, you can't take care of others if you don't take care of yourself. And second, this is YOUR life! Only *you* will live it! I'm sorry for all of the exclamation marks here, but I really need you to feel me on this. If you don't make conscious decisions about your basic needs, your desires, what's best for you, then who will? Really stop and think about that.

Choosing YOU isn't selfish; it's self-*love*. Yes, yes, that's a recycled Pinterest quote that has circulated the world—but it's also very true. Choose to prioritize yourself, and choose to change when change is necessary. If you don't like the kind of parent you are… If you don't like where you're living… If you don't like what you're doing for work… Make the decision to change. Choose a new direction. *Shift.*

And listen, I know changing anything—habits, mindset, jobs, whatever it is—it ain't easy, that's for sure. But I've actually found an insanely effective way to spark effort and build momentum. Oh man, I'm about to blow your mind with this shift in thinking. Are you sitting down? Good.

See, a lot of times when we think about who we want to be or what we want out of life, it can be kind of hard to imagine. Our minds can't even fathom this new and improved life, so we get stuck. I remember feeling this way after Rich died. I was living in pure agony and could not picture happiness or laughter in my life again.

And when we can't see it, we often freeze out of fear or doubt and don't put forth any effort. Or maybe we start and don't see immediate results, so we get frustrated with ourselves, fall off from our rigid expectations, and eventually throw in the towel. If this is you, try this…

What if instead of thinking about who you want to be, you think about who you *don't* want to be? Instead of thinking about what you want, think about what you *don't* want. When you reverse-engineer this school of thought, moving from focusing on what you want to focusing on what you *don't* want, it sparks a fire under you, and in my experience, it also brings new levels of clarity, perseverance, and intention. I'll give you an example.

After years of grinding, I was still a struggling entrepreneur, and it was dragging me into a deep depression. I was working my butt off but just felt like I couldn't "get my legs under me." It was so discouraging. When it comes to building a business—alone—the struggle is real, y'all.

Finally, something inside me snapped. I was sick and tired of being broke and feeling guilty that my son's life was limited due to my lack of consistent income. And it was even more frustrating because when I first decided to pursue the arduous journey of entrepreneurship, one of the motivating factors was to build generational wealth and not to be confined by corporate pay scales. I wanted to be in control of my income so my son would never feel the strife of a single-family income. But yet, here I was. I was under-charging because my heart is wired to give-give-give, and I was doing too much work for free, thinking it would help build my brand and generate more exposure. I'd been so modest with my fees and offerings, which made the pain of financial hardship feel suffocating.

Finally, I realized I could either choose to stay the same or I could choose to make a change.

Around that time, a friend told me something I'll never forget: "Kindness doesn't pay the bills or put food on the table," and with that in mind, I got crystal clear on my worth, my offerings, and my "that won't work for me."

I had to rewire my thinking. Instead of just setting goals and doing vision boards about the life I wanted—which yes, brought a certain amount of clarity and motivation—I jolted to a new level of grind and determination when I was sick and tired of the struggle. It ignited a different sense of urgency. I knew I didn't want to live in a state of financial stress anymore, so I changed my mindset in certain areas, adjusted a few habits, and pivoted some systems, and wouldn't ya know it—after I changed my approach, my financial strife began to change, too. This was the exact train of thought that had helped jumpstart my healing journey a few years earlier. Simply wanting to be healthy wasn't enough. Once I got in my mind that I *didn't want* to be an unhealthy mom, I simply refused to be that, and that's what helped me make deliberate decisions.

It's time to get clear, friend.

Have you ever really asked yourself, *Who do I want to be?* Really think about that. What kind of person, parent, partner, professional do you want to be? This will become your guiding compass.

I know it can feel like a heavy question, and I don't want you to feel like you have to tackle it all on your own. At the end of this chapter, you'll find an activity to help you start thinking this through by identifying your values and developing your own personal compass. When you're clear on who you want to be and who you *don't* want to be, it makes it so much easier to align your choices with being the best version of you. In fact, I'm going to encourage you to pause here and go work through that activity right now, before you move on to the next section, because it will help you get a clearer vision when we talk about making the best choices to move you toward becoming your best self.

You have the ability to define who you are and how you want to live. You can create whatever you want to create based on your choices, so be explicit and descriptive about what you want and what you don't want. Ask yourself, *Are my thoughts, habits, and behaviors supporting who I want to be?* Really look at every area of your life and see what you need to stop doing and what you need to start doing while you still can.

Our thoughts, our words, our actions shape our quality of life and the lives of others, which is why we need to choose them with care. And I'm not gonna lie—it will be difficult and uncomfortable at times to make some hard choices. But when you're determined to take your life in a new direction, you'll discover strength that you didn't know you had.

And by the way, don't you dare settle for anything other than the life you want to live.

THE RIGHT CHOICE VS. THE BEST CHOICE

You might be thinking, *How do I know what the **right** choice is?* This question creates bottlenecks in flow all the time. We wrestle with trying to make the "right" choice for a lot of reasons.

Sometimes we're trying to find a solution that will appease everyone, but the truth is it's not up to you to manage everyone else's expectations or meet every single need—especially not to the point of neglecting yourself and your needs. Trust that when you do what's best for your health and happiness, it'll cascade over into your relationships and responsibilities.

And here's a hard truth, friend: sometimes as you're making decisions that are necessary to nurture your growth, you will lose people along the way. It's tough when you have to make a decision knowing that it might be off-putting or jarring for someone else in your life, even if it's the best possible step for you personally. It can be painful, and it can make you second-guess your decisions in big ways.

Some people just will not see the best in you. And some people may not be able to celebrate your growth because they haven't found their own way yet. That has nothing to do with you and everything to do with them and the journey they're on.

That's why it's so very important to be clear about who *you* want to be and surround yourself with people who help and encourage your growth along the way. If you have people in your life who can't or won't support you with love and respect, well (read this only if you're ready to hear it), they very likely are never going to be able to embrace the person you want to become. Don't let your worries about their opinions shape your decisions. In the short term, it's only going to pull you off your path. And in the long term, it's probably just delaying the inevitable; no choice you make would ever be the right one to make them happy.

A great example of this is leaving a toxic work environment. Some people will call you irresponsible for quitting or may tell you just to suck it up, but they don't know the psychological and emotional harm being caused by your workplace. They don't know what's best for you; only you do. Outside of moral code, what's "right" is subjective. For every five people who say you're right, five people will tell you that you're wrong. If you waste precious time and energy trying to do what's right in everyone else's eyes, you will lose sight of yourself and stop trusting yourself.

Other times we look for the "right" answer that has zero margin for error. We want to make the choice that will get us to the end goal on the shortest timeline. If we're going to leave that toxic job, we want to feel absolutely sure that our next job will leave us feeling happy and fulfilled and bursting with passion every single day for the rest of our working lives. But that's just not realistic. We have to keep in mind there are always unknown factors that are out of our control. And we've got to embrace the fact that in order to evolve, we must be willing to learn along the way.

> **Instead of overthinking the *right* choice, free yourself to make the *best* choice in the moment you're in with the information you have.**

Instead of overthinking the *right* choice, which only makes you feel stuck and unproductive, free yourself to make the *best* choice in the moment you're in with the information you have. This is how you stay in flow.

Does that mean we'll be perfect? Nope, not at all. There will be times when you do your best and still fall flat on your face. But the fall will give you experience that makes you wiser, stronger, and better than you were before. That's the flex of a growth mindset—instead of having a mindset of "win or lose," you operate with the mindset of "win or learn." Remember, *all* of your experiences are molding your brain. Let me tell you something: I work hard, I don't give up, and I take responsibility for my life and choices. That's my personal best.

We're not looking to make the *right* choice when we *Shift*. All we can aim for is to make the *best* choice. Best choices are the ones that support who you want to be, the life you want to live, and the legacy you want to leave. But what does that even look like? How do you recognize the *best* choice?

> **Instead of having a mindset of "win or lose," operate with the mindset of "win or learn."**

Let's go back to that navigation app example. Let me tell you, I love a good map. I love being able to see my destination and know exactly which roads and turns and shortcuts will get me there on the fastest, most efficient route. I love having it all laid out in front of me and being able to see the journey from start to finish.

But life's not like that. We don't get turn-by-turn directions to our best lives. There is no reassuring GPS-lady voice that will let us know when we turned down a dead-end street and need to make a U-turn. There is no algorithm that will recalculate the route when it turns out that the road we're on is closed up ahead.

But even if you don't have a map, you already have what you need to get started on this journey because you, my beautiful friend, have started calibrating your compass the day you were born. (Here's where I pause to say that if you didn't turn to the end of the chapter and start working on the compass activity, *it is okay*. I promise no one is grading you here. But now that you see where I'm going with this, here's another chance to go check it out!) Your internal compass isn't designed to tell you every turn you should take. It's a tool to help you check in and make sure you're still moving in the direction of your destination.

And actually, that makes your compass way more powerful than step-by-step directions, because that compass gives you the power of *choice*. In life, we always have options—different routes to get us to our end goal. We just don't always remember to look for them. When you use your internal compass to think about the best choice, you release yourself from the pressure of trying to make the perfect decision.

Your compass lets you touch base with your values and decide how *you* want to move forward. And if it turns out your choice ended up sending you down a road that's suddenly closed ahead? That's okay, because you will find another route; you're not bound to that path forever.

Your compass keeps you moving forward. All you need to do is have confidence that when it's time to make a new decision, there will be a road available to continue the journey.

Think about the career-change example. Imagine that you clear out the noise of other people's opinions and stop worrying about trying to find the "perfect" new position. You get a job offer at a much smaller company that's known for having a really positive workplace culture. The position is a bit of a step back in title, but you know that you'll be working for an encouraging boss and in a supportive environment. You check in with your internal compass and remember that you wanted to focus on four things: being present for your kids, weeding out negativity, contributing to your community, and prioritizing your health. This new job feels like a step in the right direction for all of those goals. So you decide to take it.

Was it the right choice? *Who knows?* But it helped you move in the right direction on all of the things you value. Maybe three years from now, you'll realize you want a different kind of challenge and you'll be hunting for a new job again. That doesn't mean you made the wrong choice. In the meantime, you were able to be home every night to cook dinner and help your kids with homework and you worked with a group of people you enjoyed and respected. It doesn't matter whether it was the *right* choice. It was the *best* choice for you in that moment in your life.

The power of choice, friend—once you get that momentum, nothing can stop you. And once you start making intentional choices, keep building on that. Don't give up. When you hit hard times, choose to get back up. When you find yourself with your back up against the wall, take a beat and then choose to keep going and look for solutions.

You have to make a conscious, determined, deliberate effort to see real change in your life and in your mind. Choose how you're going to show up in every moment of every day—good times and bad. Choose your thoughts, your words, your actions. Choose your best life, and take the responsibility to make it happen.

We were all born with this superpower—the power of choice. Don't waste it; always use it wisely, because you can tie everything in your life back to a single choice. And every time you *Shift*, you're building that mental muscle that helps you align your thoughts, your words, and your actions with your best self.

YOUR PERSONAL COMPASS

Getting clear on who you are and who you want to be actually makes it much easier to make good decisions in the moment. When you pause and align your choices with the values that are important to you, then you're doing two things: you're putting your emotions in check and you're clearing out the noise in your head. Let these core qualities guide you toward mindful living. Think of them as attitudes, principles, and even mindsets that support and strengthen your best self.

An example of my guiding compass is below. On the next page, you'll find a blank compass where you can write in your own value-driven directions. There's a word bank as well in case you need some ideas to get your mind flowing. Remember, there's no right or wrong answer. It's about choosing words that matter most to you.

I've had students print this out and post it in an area they see daily so they can stay anchored in the beliefs and characteristics that are the most important to them.

Your guiding compass will likely change over time, and that's totally normal. Especially as you grow and evolve, you'll rearrange your priorities based on where you are in life. Just think about where you are today and what matters most to you now.

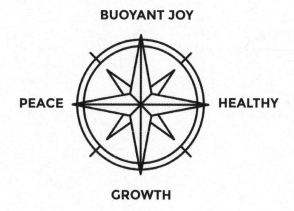

Abundance	Enlighten	Kindness	Expand	Adapt	Balance
Enjoy	Present	Less	Truth	Soul	Nourish
Alignment	Focus	Seek	Adventure	Consistency	Encourage
Learn	Grow	Mindful	Explore	Live	Dream
Flourish	Create	Flow	Bloom	Rest	Confident
Strong	Forward	Pause	Enough	Grace	Action
Boundaries	Stillness	Appreciate	Connect	Freedom	Faith
Brave	Gentle	Positivity	Alive	Calm	Conquer
Generous	Try	Simplify	Faith	Change	Release
Caring	Play	Love	Smile	Harmony	Fun
Motivate	Hope	Slow	Vulnerability	Flourish	Compassion
Dream	Thoughtful	Humble	Patience	Lead	Diligence
Intentional	Integrity	Observe	Grounded	Serve	Family
Elevate	Joy	Serenity	Be	Gratitude	Bold

> **"** *You gotta train your mind to be stronger than your emotions or else you'll lose yourself every time.* **"**

6

Things You Should Stop Doing Right Now

Did you know there's a proven equation for transformation?

Yeah, it's pretty straightforward:

$$STOP \text{ doing (and allowing) stuff that's harmful}$$
$$+ START \text{ doing things that are helpful}$$
$$= Transformation$$

If you want things to change in your life, the first step is taking inventory of the things you're allowing in your life so you can eliminate the junk that doesn't serve your happiness, your peace, or your growth.

For example, when I was in the thick of my gloom, I stopped engaging in unhelpful behavior and released everything that was toxic, negative, or harmful so that I could preserve my mental and emotional well-being.

One example of this: the news.

You may remember I said this earlier in the book, but seriously—watching the news does so much damage to our minds. I stopped watching because everything is capital-*N* Negative! As Markham Heid confirms in his article for *TIME Magazine,* "Negative news can be so intense that it can cause symptoms of acute stress—like problems sleeping, mood swings, or aggressive behavior—even PTSD."[20]

Might as well call the news the *blues* because that's how you feel after watching it. I was so happy to see John Krasinski launch his Web series *Some Good News (SGN)* during the pandemic because we needed it. From a mom and her young child befriending an elderly neighbor to generous bosses helping their employees through a tough time, *SGN* highlights only the great things going on in the world. Imagine what a difference that would make if more news outlets took this approach.

No joke, I stopped watching the news in 2013 and began tuning in, sporadically, only when the pandemic hit. Now don't get it twisted—I'm not naive and wouldn't say I live under a rock. I stopped watching the news, but I started keeping up with current events with a healthier approach.

First, I go to one of my trusted sources for reliable, yet fun, news: Trevor Noah. He covers much more than the controversial, gloomy, and discouraging stories that typically flood our airwaves. And his comic relief makes serious subjects palatable.

Second, I browse stories on my News app because it's a great way to self-curate "what's happening in the world" without being bombarded with heart-wrenching story after story, which hardwires us to be fearful and cynical.

Filtering the news helped me focus on the world around me, concentrate on things that were under my control, and spend more energy on my personal circumstances that needed my attention.

I remember the moment I made this decision. I just couldn't bear to see my husband's name and picture flash across the TV with headlines that were cold and harsh—even if they were true. I didn't need those news stories to remind me of the reality I was living in; it just intensified my pain. And not just his story—I didn't want to see *any* negative news because it exacerbated my grief.

So I cut it off.

I decided to focus my energy on my well-being and my son instead of being worried, bothered, and offended by what was on TV. I had enough stress and anxiety about what was going on in my life; I didn't want to add to it by being consumed by the worries of the world.

That's how straightforward it is to create transformation. If you want things to change, stop engaging in damaging behavior and start creating the life you want to live.

BUT FIRST, STOP OVERTHINKING

We're going to jump into some specific behaviors that need to be stopped in their tracks, but first, I just want to touch on something I know we all struggle with—overthinking.

When we set out on this personal growth journey, it always feels a little daunting at first—am I right?

Whatever the ultimate goal may be—getting unstuck and reinspired in life, losing weight, moving to a new state, leaving a draining job to pursue a meaningful career—it can be equal parts exciting and nerve-wracking. Why? Because we try to wrap our brain around every little detail that needs to happen in order to get to that final destination; and frankly, that's just way too much to figure out.

For example, say you're thinking about moving to a new city. This initial idea leads to countless other, more detailed thoughts such as:

I have to quit my job. Will my boss be disappointed? Could I transfer within the company? What if I need to find a new job? What will I do? It might be hard to establish a new network. I need to set a timeline. Between now and then I'll need to look for a place to live. Should I drive across the country or ship my car? How will I find the best neighborhood to live in? Where should I begin? This is a lot to think about…is it worth it? Maybe I should just stay. But I'm so unhappy here. Okay, where do I begin?

And more often than not, we find ourselves in a loop that is mentally exhausting.

Don't look at goals as a precise, final destination. They just help give us direction for how we want to live and who we want to be. Sometimes we get so immersed in our goals that we lose sight of enjoying the journey.

Here's the key: focus on the moment you're in right now, and make one purposeful choice one at a time. This will make everything more manageable, and your goal will feel more attainable.

Going back to the moving scenario—what if instead of letting your mind spiral out of control, you focus on one thing you can tackle in the moment? It could be as simple as researching cities online, or polishing and updating your resume, or calling a friend who lives in the area you're considering moving to for some insight on good neighborhoods.

When you do what you can in the moment you're in, other things will begin to fall into place. They always do! Blessings are already on their way to you; you just need to keep moving forward. It all starts with one choice—in the present moment.

Truthfully, friend, when I first tried to visualize my end goal of being happy again, finding internal peace, and rediscovering myself, it all felt unattainable. It was so incredibly overwhelming that the very thought of it would prevent me from taking action.

I know you've been there. We all have. And I'm telling you, take it one day, one moment, sometimes even one breath at a time. That last one was my starting point—one *breath* at a time.

Overthinking hinders the momentum you need to grow forward. When you notice yourself spiraling, gently bring yourself back to the present moment. You can do this by focusing on your breath, going for a walk, or even sitting in nature. Breaking it down to the very moment you're in will help instantly relieve anxiety and worry. When your mind is free from those distractions, you'll have more energy, clarity, and a stronger desire to take healthy action and grow.

A little progress each day adds up to big results. There is no quick fix or rapid-fire approach to change. It takes discipline, perseverance, and a positive attitude.

IT'S A HUMAN THING

I think it was when I was sitting next to a widow who was sharing the story of losing her husband to cancer and literally watching the last breath leave his body when I realized our pain may be packaged differently, but the feeling is the same.

For all of us. We all know what it's like to feel pain. We all struggle with the same internal battles like stress, doubt, regret, anxiety…and these things weigh heavy on our minds. They're normal and natural emotions, but we've got to do a better job of managing them.

Instead of trying to create a problem-free life, we need to focus our energy on building a strong, healthy mindset to navigate whatever comes our way.

The more you grow, the more you flow.

If you can reframe your thinking and choose a positive response, ultimately you'll learn how to flow with life. Your growth mindset will help you develop grit, which will give you the strength to get through small and big challenges.

I wanted to focus the second part of this book on the five most common negative thought cycles that can trip us up:

1. Stress
2. Self-doubt
3. Dwelling on the past
4. Feeling anxious
5. Neglecting your needs

Now let me be crystal clear: this isn't a magic trick. I'm not saying *Stop & Shift* will bring a halt to all of those things; we're human and our emotions are complex. But it's undoubtedly a tool that will help you flow with emotions, disruptions, and challenges so you're not stuck in an unhealthy thought cycle for too long.

These are just a few common life experiences that can hold us back from living a full life if we don't manage them properly. And here's a healthier way to start looking at those tough, trying times: they're practice. Start looking at *every* disruptive moment as an opportunity to practice these skills, flex your mental strength, and reset your mindset. Instead of holding on to a sour attitude about an unfavorable situation, take a deep breath and practice *Stop & Shift* every chance you get, my friend. The more you grow, the more you flow.

MY MENTAL BARRIERS

What other mental barriers are preventing you from living a full life? Write down any negative thoughts that you want to *Stop* and *Shift* away from; we will work on shifting these later in the book.

Spend five to ten minutes focusing on your thoughts to strengthen your brain. Don't skip this! Even if you can't think of any additional negative thoughts to write down, simply spending the next few minutes tuning in to what's running through your head will strengthen your mind through stillness and concentration.

_____

_____

_____

_____

_____

_____

_____

_____

_____

_____

_____

_____

_____

_____

_____

_____

_____

_____

_____

_____

_____

_____

_____

_____

_____

_____

_____

_____

_____

_____

_____

_____

_____

_____

_____

By the way, I love hearing stories about how you use Stop & Shift so puh-lease, as you're reading this and applying it to your life → POST about it, share your mental strength-training journey (the good and the bad; let's keep it real, friend), and tag me so I can cheer you on from the sidelines! Use #StopAndShift when you post so I can find you.

PART 2

SHIFT

> **" It is what it is. It was what it was. It will be what it will be. Don't stress about it. "**

7

Stress Sucks

Stress has a large impact on our mental well-being and can manifest in physical ways if we don't learn how to manage it.

When we try to suppress or ignore stress, it can trigger intense headaches, elevate our blood pressure, and cause insomnia, stomachaches, digestive issues, and much, much more. Left unmanaged, stress has more severe long-term side effects, like increased risk of heart attack and a weakened immune system—leaving you susceptible to getting sick more often and putting you at greater risk for chronic diseases.

The good news is, the better we get at managing smaller disruptions and stressors in life, the stronger we are when the time comes to navigate the big stuff. The stress that comes with losing a spouse is indescribable. The stress of losing your car, house, and job is also overwhelming. And when you pile these on top of one another, what do you get?

Complete and utter chaos.

That's what happened in the first year after losing Richard. Yep, I lost all those things and more. Guess you could say it was a year from hell.

The last Band-Aid that was ripped off was losing my job. It was a Monday. I walked into the office after a pretty emotional weekend. The Friday before, I'd just closed on selling our home—the house Richard and I bought together. The biggest purchase of our lives, the achievement that made us feel like "real" adults, was now also a milestone tied to his sudden death.

Moving into that house was the beginning of us building our lives and our family together. Selling it was a stark reality check that life was completely different now. I couldn't afford the house, and it was too big for just Caleb and me, not to mention I felt like I was suffocating in there because every corner of the house reminded me of the life that Richard and I had been excited to build together.

So while it was a practical move, it wasn't an easy decision to make alone. Moving into a new home was bittersweet. I wasn't ready to close that chapter of my life, but the new space felt like fresh oxygen—like a cornerstone on this journey of rebuilding my life.

With all the changes happening around me, I was trying to feel hopeful about the future and focus on things to be grateful for—like having a stable job.

And really, that's what was saving me and helping me get through each day—that shift into my gratitude attitude. Gratitude for something like having a stable job is macro level.

But sometimes I had to get down to the micro level. I would stop myself and sink into my gratitude for my soft pillow or a full belly after a meal.

I didn't have a word for it at the time, but later I realized that what I was doing was practicing mindfulness. I told you, mindfulness isn't just meditation. Listen, if meditation works for you, it's a great tool, but mindfulness is really just about finding strategies to ground yourself in the present moment.

That's what I was doing when I was giving thanks for soft pillows and full bellies. The future and the past felt overwhelming, but if I could dig in and get really clear about what was good in the present moment, I could find some peace.

When I walked into the office the following Monday morning, I hit the ground running with work. I hopped on the phone with a hiring manager to negotiate a salary offer that we'd been working on for a candidate, which also needed the final approval from our HR director. On my way to find her, she found me and said we needed to chat. I assumed it was regarding this high-level position that we were working on. I had no idea what was to come...

When I walked into her office, my boss was on speakerphone—which surprised me because it was about 5:30 a.m. his time; he worked out of our corporate office in Scottsdale, Arizona.

They proceeded to tell me that I was being let go—effective immediately.

I was instantly overwhelmed with disbelief. I don't remember their exact words, but I remember how I felt...abandoned.

I felt like my boss and I had a great, transparent relationship. He was incredibly compassionate after Richard died, and he later shared with me that this was because he had a near-death experience with his wife, so he'd had a glimpse of what it felt like to be in my shoes. Because of this, he helped make sure I had an extended bereavement period so I could work through the immediate shock. He also advocated for me to work from home part-time for the first few months so I could go to therapy and get Caleb adjusted to daycare.

I truly appreciated his high level of consideration because when you're grieving the death of someone close to you, the last thing you want to be worried about is job security.

And in this place, they would let people go in a heartbeat without rhyme or reason. Our workplace was a "burn 'em and turn 'em" environment. No one was safe—from folks high up on the totem pole down to the worker bees and everyone in between.

Being very aware of the culture, I specifically said to my boss on several occasions, "If I'm ever in danger of losing my job, please give me a heads-up. Now, as a single parent, I can't be left out to dry like that. I don't know what I'd do." He reassured me that all was well and if anything were to change, he'd let me know. And I had faith that he would.

After losing Rich, it took me several months, but I was finally able to find my flow again. I was hitting all my goals, performing to the best of my ability. So a year later, in the midst of crushing it, the possibility of losing my job wasn't even a thought.

That morning, as I sat there receiving this terrible news, I was crushed. Devastated. Completely hopeless. After all I'd been through that year, this was a total slap in the face. I walked back into my office, packed up a little box of my belongings, held back tears as best I could while walking to my car, and once the door was shut and the radio on, I started bawling.

The stress of life felt unbearable at this point—I was completely broken. Every negative thought you can imagine ran through my head:

I am an absolute loser.

I am unemployed with no savings.

I'm failing my son; I'm a horrible mother.

I can't live like this anymore—not knowing what bad news is waiting to drop on me like a bomb.

Needless to say, I was crushed, angry, sad, mortified…and rightly so! Over and over, I kept saying to myself, *What am I going to do? Now what?* But then, in a matter of minutes, I started shifting my mindset to pull myself out of despair and hopelessness.

What am I going to do? turned from being a question full of frustration to a question full of hope and possibility. I transformed my destructive thoughts into new thoughts to help adjust my perspective on the situation.

Instead of *I am an absolute loser,* I reminded myself, *I've been doing the best I can. And numbers don't lie, I was crushing my goals.*

Instead of *I am unemployed with no money,* I reminded myself, *I have a few weeks of severance to figure it out.*

Instead of *I'm failing my son,* I reminded myself, *He's safe, happy, and loved.*

Instead of *I can't live like this anymore,* I reminded myself, *What an opportunity to rest and reset.*

Now, I'm not saying I never experienced those woe-is-me thoughts again. But every time they crept in to take over my mind, I'd choose to shift to a more positive and productive thought. As the saying goes, there's no point in crying over spilled milk. I couldn't change the fact that I was let go, but

I could choose how I was going to respond to this news; the year from hell taught me that lesson.

So as I sat there in my car, wiping away my tears, I started thinking about my options. And I realized, what felt like a slap in the face was actually the push I needed to change directions.

See, my soul had already been yearning for something different—a life and a career that would provide me the freedom and flexibility to put my son first. Because as a single parent, I never wanted to miss a moment when he needed me: a school function, a call from the nurse, what have you. I can't miss anything; I'm the only parent he has.

And let's keep it real, most companies aren't very understanding when it comes to the harsh realities that come with being a single parent.

> What felt like a slap in the face was actually the push I needed to change directions.

So in that moment, when I adjusted my outlook on what had just happened, I felt *relieved* instead of offended. Like a weight had been lifted. I didn't know exactly what I was going to do or how I was going to do it, but I gave myself a time frame to figure it out. And over the next few weeks, I started to put a plan in place.

Have I wanted to give up along the way? Sure. This entrepreneurial road ain't easy, that's for sure. But my "why," the center of all my decisions— my son—helps me remember the reason I started. And he's why I haven't given up.

Now, while losing a job is a pretty big example of stress, let's be real— more often than not, we're stressed about a whole bunch of little stuff. Fussing about and dwelling on little things that are out of our control, like a change of plans, a broken toilet, a hectic day; the list goes on and on.

If you get bent out of shape about every little thing, you'll constantly be frustrated and stressed by life. But if you learn how to flow with life's ups and downs, you'll experience less stress and more joy. The little stuff just isn't worth it.

Here's an everyday example: traffic…

THE TRAFFIC 'TUDE

Imagine you're driving down the street, probably lost in thought or listening to a song. You switch lanes without realizing you forgot to use your turn signal. All of a sudden, there's a minivan blaring its horn behind you, and you can see the woman in the driver's seat throwing her hands wildly in the air. And wait, was that THE finger?

This angered woman switches lanes so she can pull up next to you and give you the deadliest stare down e-v-e-r. Everything she was yelling while behind you, she's now mouthing while she sees she has your attention.

It doesn't end there.

She speeds up, only to *cut you off* without using *her* turn signal!

Now your body is filled with rage; you're yelling back, hands are flying, you're even looking for something in your car to throw at the minivan. Stress is ignited and heightened in a matter of seconds, and for both drivers, the stress doesn't melt away quickly. It's taken with you to your destination, into your next interaction—with coworkers, kids, spouse, etc.…and it could even ruin the rest of your day.

Let's break down how you could shift your mindset in this scenario…

First, let's start with the driver of the minivan. I'll admit, it's easy to get ticked off by a careless driver or the occasional intentional arsehole. Part of the problem is that we tend to make these frustrating moments really personal. Instead of acknowledging that we all have moments where we're not the best drivers, that we've all had a time when our mind was on something else and we forgot to check our blind spot, or when we suddenly had to pull over right then and there because our kiddo was about to have a bathroom emergency, or…

You get the idea. But on the other end, in the moment, we personalize it—"That driver cut me off"—even though we know from our own personal experience that it probably has nothing to do with us. But once it's personal, it's so much more difficult for us to let it go.

The first step is just noticing that you're angry. Or frustrated. Or annoyed. Sometimes we act based on a flood of emotions. But the only way to step back from those transient emotions is to get really clear on what we're feeling. Once you're focused on the actual emotion that's coming up, it's easier to shift away from that negativity.

And then you make a choice. An intentional choice. When you move into that space, you're not making snap decisions based on emotions that ebb and flow. You're not just reacting to the situation you're currently in. You're thinking and feeling through and making an intentional choice that will serve you and the people around you. You could start by taking your foot off the pedal to slow down, and while doing so, you could say to yourself:

I want to go off, but do I really want to feel all that stress and negative energy? Let me back off and create some space so we don't get in an accident. I'm definitely not going to let some random, careless driver ruin my mood. Plus, what I say isn't going to affect them. I'm in the car by myself. Not to mention, I can't do anything to change what's already happened. *deep breaths*

Now, the careless driver. Let's just keep it real—we've all been this person who accidentally cut off another car. Given that you can't control the other person who's going off in the minivan, you can still play a role in defusing the situation in order to repel any negative energy. Instead of getting caught up in the heated back and forth, take a breath and atone your mishap. Shift the energy with the opposite emotion by giving a gentle wave and apology. *deep breaths**

Now you're not carrying the weight of that interaction or another person's negativity the rest of your day, so you get to show up as your best self in your interactions.

STANKNESS

Another common stressor is other people's attitudes. Stress can frequently be triggered by someone else's bad mood, bitter behavior, or overall toxic energy.

I told you that when I was first starting my healing journey, one of the things I decided I needed to do was cut out anything that would add to my pain or bring more toxicity into my life. That's something I carried forward. I have zero tolerance for negative energy in my space. In fact, I use it as a guidepost when I make decisions big and small. If the result will be bringing negative energy into my life, it's a hard *no* for me.

Sometimes that means making big decisions about who and what I keep in my life. Working toward that balance started when I was in the depths of my grief.

I realized I needed to take inventory. I had to get really clear about what I was making room for in my life because I was either going to choose to hold space for things that were harmful or I was going to choose to hold space for things that were healthy. When you know what you no longer want to hold space for in your life, you can start to develop habits that will allow you to keep them from creeping in. And then you can start to seek out tools to help you build those habits.

That's how you can choose how you're showing up. It all starts with awareness.

At the time, I would suppress uncomfortable emotions or thoughts because I believed if I went there, I wouldn't have a way back out again. I thought the hurt would be unbearable. I thought it would take me out. Instead, I just tried to avoid the dark places and the discomfort.

What I realized, though, was when I was able to stand in the discomfort, it actually bolstered my power, because I could face the negative emotions and also make room for hope and positive possibilities. I could find my way out.

I get asked this question a lot: "How do I protect myself (and my mind) from someone's negative behavior or rude attitude, especially if they're someone close to me—like a family member or someone I work with?"

I'll be honest, it takes practice, but it is possible. Here's what I do:

Step One

First, I take a beat so I don't allow my emotions to drive my reaction to the situation. During that pause, I remind myself that I don't know everything this person is going through—and everyone's going through something.

See, usually when someone is bringing toxic energy to the table, it rarely has anything to do with you and everything to do with the hurt and pain they're carrying. Remember how I said we personalize everything?

Reminding myself of this helps me not to take their behavior so personally or get defensive. It also softens my heart to feel empathy for whatever they're going through—whether I know the details or not.

Details don't really matter because I know what pain feels like; we all do. Our problems may be packaged differently, but the pain is the same.

Step Two

After checking in with myself, I decide if I'm going to engage or not. I can't control how they're acting, but I can control how I choose to show up.

> Our problems may be packaged differently, but the pain is the same.

This is important to remember, so get your highlighter out: *you're responsible only for your behavior, how you respond to life, and how you treat other people.*

Step Three

Here's the key if you do choose to engage: *bring the light.* Don't let their bad attitude rub off on you.

Be pleasant, kind, and show love. Darkness can't live where light is. When you bring the light, it may not change how people are acting, but it will certainly protect your heart from the darkness.

And if you choose not to engage, then you also have to choose to leave their stankness with them. When you replay their unpleasantries in your head over and over, you're carrying their baggage with you throughout the day. Friend, let me remind you, it's not yours to carry.

Shifting from stress takes both time and practice. But the good news is, there are a lot of opportunities throughout the day to build this mental muscle. Micro-stressors are everywhere, and when you practice shifting from them, you're training your brain to remain composed and not react to or be offended by every little glitch, flaw, or mishap.

I've been lost in tears and have had the kind of stress in my chest that makes it hard to breathe, let alone think. But I can sit in those feelings. I go deep. I've found strength in those hard places. I can go there *and* shift. That's the goal. We don't shift to ignore—we shift so we don't remain stuck!! Practice flowing with minor disruptions in life and try not to stay stuck in the negative thought cycle for too long. The more you do this, the easier it gets.

SHIFT YOUR STRENGTH

Write down two things you've been stressing about lately (on the left side of the page).

Write down thoughts or actions to shift those stressors (on the right side of the page).

" Thoughts can be such bullies. Stand up to them. Know your truth."

8

Doubt Is a Distraction

Doubt usually creeps up when we're doing something new, brave, or big. Doubt is real, but it's also a major distraction.

It can create a false reality in your mind that will hold you back from growth, new experiences, and living fully. It's an internal battle that we all go through, but it's up to you whether you're going to let it hold you prisoner in your own mind.

In my opinion, doubt can be one of the easier negative thought cycles to move through—once you start calling its bluff. You just have to break the cycle of believing the doubt and start believing in yourself.

Yes, it takes time, and it takes practice, but once you see doubt for what it really is—empty energy—you won't let it linger for too long. Trust me, this was one of the biggest hurdles I had to learn how to get over because of all the uncertainty that comes with being an entrepreneur.

When I was let go from my job, I was literally starting from ground zero: no business plan, no seed money, just following my heart and talking to God. I really didn't know exactly what I was going to do or how I was going to do it, so you can believe I was totally consumed with doubt. And not just in the first few days or months…doubt followed me for years until I learned how to get a grip on it.

I vividly remember one moment when I felt like I was drowning in doubt.

I was driving to a networking event about 45 minutes from my house. On my way there, my mind started racing with uncertainty and worry. My lack of confidence was at an all-time high because I wasn't as far along in my career as I wanted to be—and I wanted to get there faster.

Then I started spiraling downward, telling myself how stupid I was to chase a dream of being an entrepreneur. At this point, I'd been on the journey for two years, and I felt like I was going nowhere. Not to mention the pressure I was putting on myself and the very real financial struggle, which felt like it had me in a relentless headlock.

My eyes were flooded with tears, and when I couldn't hold them back any longer, they started rolling down my face at a rapid rate. This was no time for a breakdown, not on the way to an event, but I just couldn't help it. My heart was heavy.

I didn't know what to do, so I cried out to God:

I don't know if I'm on the right path. I'm scared. I don't know how to make this work. Am I wasting time? Am I on the wrong path? How do I know if I'm chasing silly dreams or I'm really pursuing what you've put in my heart? I'm so confused; I don't know if I can keep doing this.

Let me pause for a moment to explain one of my core beliefs: I wholeheartedly believe that we're all uniquely created and each of us has been given a heart for something special, along with the talents and abilities to do meaningful work. When we follow the desires of our heart, that's how we know we're living out our purpose. And I realize "purpose" can be a heavy word, but it really doesn't have to be so deep.

Someone who has a heart for animals and is really interested in medicine may find their purpose as a vet. Someone who is really good at writing and has a heart for music could be a songwriter.

My point is, we're all created in different ways to contribute to this world. But oftentimes we suppress this calling because it's not practical or we've been told to pursue a more standard, safe, status quo life.

Once I realized how short life is, I felt a strong pull to find my purpose and do work that matters.

So in this particular moment, when I was crying out to God, frustrated and full of doubt, I begged for two signs: one, a hallmark speaking gig that would confirm I'm meant to be a professional speaker.

To be honest, I never wanted to be a speaker; it wasn't a dream of mine or anything. But after losing Richard and losing my job, I felt like I was being led in that direction. So I just wanted a little confirmation from the Creator of the Universe to know if I was on the right path or not.

I specifically remember praying, *If this is your will, no matter how long it takes, I'll be patient. But I just gotta at least know if I'm on the right path.*

The second thing I prayed for was my first corporate client. I'd designed training workshops to educate employers on how to manage grief in the workplace with compassion and empathy. But I had yet to land my first paying client. So I asked God, *If this content is needed in the world, please send me my first corporate partner.*

Oh, and I asked for answers to these doubts by March.

(Haha, I know you're probably reading this and thinking, "Girl, you're crazy." But hey, I'm not ashamed to tell you I pray some *bold* prayers when I'm talking to my Heavenly Papa. And I talk to him just like I talk to anyone; I keep it REAL.)

Now the point of this story isn't to suggest God is a genie—that's not how it works. But in that moment of complete distress, while en route to a networking party, I had to choose how I was going to process and work through those thoughts so I could get myself together.

I allowed myself to go there, to that broken place, and give words to what I was feeling—doubtful.

Even though I could barely see the road through those heavy tears, my prayers were therapeutic and comforting and, most of all, they gave me space to release my doubts so they weren't suffocating me.

After that heartfelt prayer, I took a long, deep breath—and released the outcome. I decided to trust that my answer was on the way. I accepted that it wasn't going to come in the next few minutes. And I chose to still go to the networking event instead of isolating myself.

Let me point out, there's no magic trick to feeling better instantly. Your power lies in making a conscious decision about how you respond to the doom when it starts to feel too heavy to handle. The choice is yours.

So, are you wondering what happened—whether my prayers were answered or not?

Well, the next couple of months weren't all sunshine and rainbows. That's for sure. But I did get my answers in March...

With regard to the hallmark speaking gig, well, I was invited to do a TEDx talk. Talk about a positive sign! And yes, I received a contract for my first *paid* workshop with a corporate partner. Whoop! Whoop! *cue the confetti and pop the champagne* So so exciting.

But let me be totally transparent with you, friend. These incredibly awesome opportunities didn't blow up my career. They didn't launch me into "overnight success" territory.

Nope.

But they did give me the answers I was looking for. And remember, I said in my prayer, *I'll be patient. I just need a sign, a little encouragement, to know I'm headed in the right direction.*

I meant that. And after this experience, I stopped doubting as much. I still had some rocky moments, but they were less intense and were short-lived. Because from that point on, whenever I did doubt my purpose, I reminded myself of that answered prayer and every other sign that's come across my path to keep me on course.

Having a relationship with God is what holds me together, and I'm not here to preach to you about what to believe, but when you're doubting that you're on the right path, trust the "positive omens."*

As a God-girl, I call those #GodHugs.

---

*The concept of "positive omens" comes from my all-time favorite book, *The Alchemist*, by Paulo Coelho (New York: HarperOne, 1988).

Doubt will rear its ugly head when your soul is yearning for more. Pay attention to that and notice when you need to overcome doubt with faith; just follow the positive omens.

> "In order to find the treasure, you will have to follow the omens. God has prepared a path for everyone to follow. You just have to read the omens that he left for you."
>
> –Paulo Coelho, *The Alchemist*[21]

There's so much we can take from this excerpt, but for now I want to point out how the author suggests that faith is what enables us to overcome doubt and find the treasure that's rightfully ours. This has been so true in my life, and I've also seen it in the lives of others. Faith as tiny as a grain of salt or a mustard seed can help you shed the layers of doubt little by little until you feel freed from that bondage.

The author also connects doubt to our desire for more out of life. Like I said earlier, it usually comes up when we're about to do something new, brave, or big.

TAKE A FLYING LEAP

Have you ever wanted to do something big? I mean really big. Like, so big you felt silly telling anyone about it. Sooo big it was scary. Soooo big that as soon as you felt excitement at the thought of it, you were simultaneously filled with doubt. Those moments of doubt should be a sign that whatever you're about to embark on is going to require a bit of faith and bravery.

Let me tell you about my friend Erin. She'd been in her corporate job for twenty years, a job she loved; she even went to grad school with aspirations of using that degree to do higher-level work within the organization.

But something started to shift in her soul. Maybe it was the crappy management or bureaucratic red tape or lack of support or maybe it was everything together, but week after week, she became more unsettled with where she was in life. It grew to be so intense that she could no longer ignore this desire for more.

You know that feeling. We've all had it. It's just that most people suppress it because they cave to doubt instead of leaning into exploring their authentic self.

Stephen Cope's book *The Great Work of Your Life* was my first introduction to *dharma*, which is your life's work.[22] Not just a job or a career, but the thing that pairs in harmony with your natural gifts, interests, and also serves humanity. When you're tapped into this, you're lit up! But one of the main barriers that often stands in the way of living out your *dharma* is doubt. You feel unsure of exactly what to do or how to do it, and then if you add other people's doubt and opinions into the mix, that can really cloud your vision. Or maybe you're unsure if you deserve that life that you're dreaming of—maybe you think it's too good to be true or the dream is too far out of reach. That's common when you love the work you do and you can't imagine someone paying you for having fun, being in flow, or doing what you love to do.

> When we doubt ourselves, we abandon ourselves.

The problem is, when we doubt ourselves, we abandon ourselves. We ignore what feels right in our gut. It makes us feel split between two worlds: the one where we feel stuck and unfulfilled, and the other that's waiting for us if only we would make the time to know ourselves, love ourselves, and trust ourselves. As

I was reading *The Great Work of Your Life*, the word *dharma* transcended work and came into focus as a way of living, a way of *being*. Being true to yourself in all areas of life.

I also fell in love with the term *ikigai* (pronounced "ee-key-guy"). The *Oxford English Dictionary* defines *ikigai* as "a motivating force; something or someone that gives a person a sense of purpose or a reason for living."[23] Japanese culture suggests that everyone has an *ikigai*—a real purpose in life. There's a Japanese village with the world's longest-living people who will tell you that finding it is the key to a happier and longer life (the graphic below shows how to find your *ikigai*).

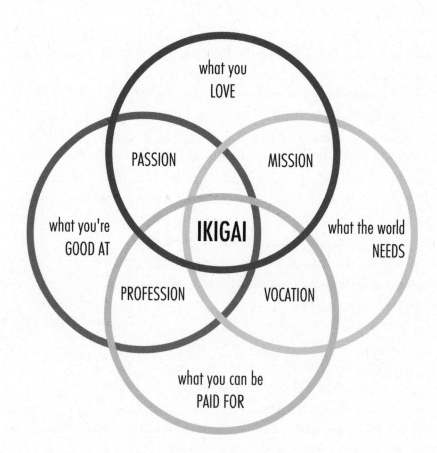

Whatever you want to call it, doubt is the number-one killer of dharma, ikigai, and optimal living. I love this statement from Cope: "You can only expect a fulfilling life if you dedicate yourself to finding out *who you are*."[24]

Maybe pause for a second, friend, and ask yourself, *Am I living fully right now?* If the answer is *no*, then first of all, that's okay because this is just your starting point. Now it's time to *Stop* letting doubt limit your life and instead *Shift* to positive thoughts and healthy actions that align with who you want to be and the life you deserve. Remember, every time you *Shift* from doubt, you're rewiring your brain with faith. When you choose to break free from doubt, you're proving that the world around you doesn't control you; you control who you want to be in the world.

So, if you're wondering what happened to Erin…

Well, it's a pretty awesome story—one that I hope she writes in a book someday. The short version is, she pushed through self-doubt, cashed in her retirement, and started her next chapter in a new state. She'll tell you it was the best decision of her life. She's less stressed, more confident, and healthier than she's ever been before—physically, mentally, emotionally, and spiritually. She's met the most amazing group of humans along her adventures of surfing, hiking, meditating, surrendering, and exploring. Now, she's using her gifts to help other women who are in transition and looking for guidance on how to create a more balanced, holistic lifestyle. She doesn't have a five-to-ten-year plan, but that's okay because she became boldly intentional about creating the right conditions that would allow her to flourish. When I think about Erin's journey, I think of a quote by country-western singer Dolly Parton: "Find out who you are and then do it on purpose."[25] I believe without a shadow of doubt that is the blueprint to a meaningful life.

IT'S IMPOSSIBLE—OR IS IT?

Nick Vujicic is an incredible—*absolutely incredible*—human. His name may not be familiar, but his story may be. Nick is a motivational speaker who has no arms and no legs. That's right, he was born with no limbs.

In his TED talk, which has reached over six million viewers, he shares the internal battle he struggled with as a child, how the negative thoughts were so loud and discouraging that he wanted to give up on life.

You're not good enough.
You're never going to get a job.
You won't get married; you couldn't even hold your wife's hand.
What kind of father would be? You couldn't even hold your child.

The doubts were so rampant in his head—escalated by the bullying he faced at school—that at only eight years old, he contemplated suicide. And then at age ten, he actually tried to end his life, attempting to drown himself in the bathtub at home. Then his mind shifted, and one thought saved his life: he didn't want his fatal decision to be a burden on his parents.

According to Nick, the victory over his struggles, as well as his strength and passion for life today, can be credited to his faith. Since his first speaking engagement at age nineteen, Nick has traveled around the world, sharing his story with millions, sometimes in stadiums filled to capacity, speaking to a range of diverse groups such as students, teachers, young people, business professionals, and church congregations of all sizes.

Today, this dynamic young evangelist has accomplished more than most people achieve in a lifetime. He's an author, musician, actor, and his hobbies include fishing, painting, and swimming.

I think anyone would understand if someone with Nick's physical limitations lived consumed by doubt. Doubting their purpose, doubting their abilities, doubting their future, and everything else. But if Nick had listened to those doubts, if he'd hidden behind his physical impairments, he wouldn't be inspiring and changing millions of people's lives.

I loved learning about Nick and hearing his story because he's a great example that nothing is impossible, even if it seems to be. Doubt could have stifled him, hopelessness could've killed him, but his faith helped him overcome these negative thought cycles, and now his life is *full*, in spite of his perceived limitations. Nick said in his TED talk: "Even if you don't get a miracle, you can be a miracle for someone else."[26] This is so true.

Don't let doubt distract you from your destiny. Have faith, be brave, and follow the positive omens.

LEARNING TO RIDE OUT THE STORMS

The highs and lows of life are where we can really get stuck. When we're riding a high, it's hard to imagine that we'll ever come down from it, and when we hit a low, it's hard to see how we'll ever rise back up. So how do you navigate those changes?

Let me tell you about my friend Ryan Campbell. When Ryan was a teenager, he set a goal that makes me look back at my teenage self and think, *Girl, you were kind of slacking...* When Ryan was fifteen, he flew solo for the first time. Yep, flew. While lots of us were still figuring out parallel parking, my guy Ryan was up in the air.

And then when he was seventeen, he found out that the youngest person ever to fly solo around the world had been twenty-three. His reaction to that factoid is epic as far as I'm concerned: he thought, *Okay, so that means I've got six years to beat the record.*

Amazing, right?

So he set to work to fundraise, plan, and train for his adventure. And at nineteen, he became the youngest person (and the first teenager!) to fly solo around the world. He was named one of Australia's 50 Great Explorers. He met Prince William and Buzz Aldrin. He wrote a book about his adventures. Can you imagine a bigger high?

And then his life changed in a heartbeat.

Two years after his round-the-world flight, Ryan was involved in a devastating plane crash. He suffered a serious spinal cord injury, multiple breaks in his back, and broken bones throughout his body. In an instant, he lost the use of his legs. He spent six months in the hospital and a year and a half in rehabilitation. Not only did he have to give up his passion, flying, he had to learn to walk again.

Hearing his story, you could just imagine how easy it would've been for Ryan to get swallowed up by that low.

But you know what? He didn't.

Instead, he found a moment where he could stop his internal negative narrative about the unfairness of his situation and focus on one positive idea that would help him shift into a new mindset and fuel his healing, physically and mentally.

In his first physical rehabilitation session, Ryan was working through the first task the therapists put before him—rolling over on his own. He loved a good challenge, and he was ready! But then, as he was twisted around, trying to figure out how to accomplish the task, he experienced a huge surge of pain and stopped to catch his breath. While he was resting, he noticed another patient across the room who'd sustained an injury that left him a quadriplegic, with no movement below his chest. He was in the middle of his own rehabilitation exercise, which was moving his arms in and out a few inches at a time.

And Ryan suddenly realized that as painful as this moment was for him, as frustrating as he might find the challenges he faced, he was profoundly lucky to be struggling with rolling over. It was a huge mountain to climb, but he had the opportunity to do it, something that this other patient might not.

So he mentally locked into the feeling he had in the moment. He stopped an internal dialogue that was focused on everything he'd lost and shifted his focus toward growth. He decided that as he worked on his physical healing, he'd also unpack his experiences to focus on his own mental growth; he could see that learning to walk again would be a mental journey as much as a physical one. He could track his physical growth, but it was so much harder to track mental growth. He'd really unpack the lessons he learned in each moment so that he could carry them forward into any new challenge he faced.

And even if I stopped the story right there, I think we could agree that his determination and resilience in the face of huge challenges is pretty incredible.

But as he healed, Ryan realized he had an opportunity to go even further— to help others discover their capacity for growth and resilience. Here's what he told me about what he hopes his experiences can teach other people: "The storms are always there, they always will be, and they are actually fuel for incredible success and an incredible future if we are willing to grab hold of it."

Today, after years of work and growth, Ryan is an amazing public speaker who teaches other people how to develop their own resilience. And he's back to flying again.

Every time you refuse to give up—every time you make the choice to get up instead—you build your resilience. The storms don't get smaller. You learn from each one, and then you get better at flying through them.

DREAM BIGGER

Write down something you want to accomplish in your life. It doesn't have to be work related; it can be anything your soul is yearning for but you've put on the back burner because it doesn't seem possible. Put all of the details down on paper; don't leave anything out.

_____

_____

_____

_____

_____

_____

_____

_____

_____

Write down WHY you want this dream. Think about what's at the core of your desires.

_____

_____

_____

_____

_____

_____

_____

_____

_____

What doubts get stirred up when you think about pursuing this idea?

_____

_____

_____

_____

_____

_____

_____

_____

_____

_____

Now imagine you're talking to a friend with this dream and s/he just rattled off these doubts—what would you say to motivate him/her? Write down your advice, guidance, and encouragement.

_____

_____

_____

_____

_____

_____

_____

_____

_____

_____

_____

_____

> **" Don't be a prisoner of your past. It was a lesson, not a life sentence. "**
>
> —Robin Sharma

9

Dwelling on the Past

Often when we go through a stressful time or hardship, we ruminate on negative baggage from our past.

Something someone said to us.
A missed opportunity.
A mistake or moment of failure.

Dwelling on the past can be really dangerous because over time, you lose perspective on the present reality. This is classic self-destruction.

Don't worry, I'm not judging. I've spent some time in that fortress, and that's why I'm bringing it up to you here. Because I know how toxic it can be.

I couldn't stop thinking about the past, even though life kept trying to push me forward.

You know, the first week after someone dies is unexpectedly busy. Even though you're in shock, feeling numb, and running on autopilot, you have to take care of "business"—i.e., funeral arrangements, medical examiner's office, death certificates, insurance (if you have some; we did not), kids' needs, family needs, work needs, etc. For the record, it's immensely difficult to make confident decisions when your mind is clouded and overwhelmed with complex emotions.

Not to mention, I had reporters coming to my door, wanting statements about what had happened. Thankfully, I had friends and family who shielded me from this insensitive behavior, but it didn't shield me from the thoughts that loomed—my husband's killer was still out there.

I just want to pause and call out employers who only give three to five days off for bereavement—this is ridiculous and needs to change. Thankfully, my boss went above and beyond to get company-wide donated time off. Many aren't as fortunate, and that's why we need *policies* in place to protect our well-being.

And in the midst of all this chaos, I was obsessing over every little detail about his murder in my head.

I wish I'd gotten out of the car to give him a proper goodbye, to hug him.

Why'd I have to take that call from work?

What if the kids had been there?

Had his killer been watching us?

Was it really random?

Did Rich see it coming?

Was he scared?

Did I miss anything as a wife?

The repetitive thoughts consumed my mind, all day and all night. All of these details about what could've happened, what should've happened, "if only" this and that. I couldn't think about anything else. I couldn't think about eating, washing my face, what to do next, work…I was just lost in a fog of the past.

I called the detectives regularly, wanting answers. And each time I picked up the phone, scrolled through to find the number, waited while the phone rang, I felt terribly sick. I eventually started spacing out how often I would call because the wave of sickness was becoming more and more debilitating. It was more than feeling anxious; it was feeling like I had to remain in the fetal position leading up to the call and then feeling the same sickness after hearing there was no update and they were no closer to solving the case.

Finally, after a few months of this downward spiral, I knew I had to make a difficult, but necessary, decision. I had to let the police do their job and trust that whenever they had something to report, they would call me. I remember battling guilt and feeling like I was giving up on Rich. I worried that if I wasn't calling and texting the detectives, they would care less about his case.

And along those same lines, I had to let go of the things in the past that were out of my control. The hug I didn't get, the what-ifs that may never have an answer, and the moments I was replaying over and over in my head became pure torture. The internal struggle was intense, but finally, I realized I couldn't be fully present for my son and do what I needed to do to heal if I was obsessing over things I couldn't change.

It was in this season that I learned a life-changing lesson about acceptance. I started to better understand what it means to truly accept the things that are out of my control.

In our society, we often view acceptance as a sign of consent, or that whatever happened is justified—which isn't always true.

Let me say this again: when you accept something, that doesn't mean you're okay with it. I had to accept that my husband died, but I sure as heck was NOT okay with it. Acceptance isn't a rite of passage; it's a choice to release what you can't change. When you accept what's happened, you're simply acknowledging your starting point and where you are in the present moment so you can choose how you're going to respond and move forward.

Acceptance doesn't have to mean approval.

There is so much freedom on the other side of acceptance. And I'm not saying accepting harsh realities from your past is easy, but it's *way* better than feeling weighed down by the bad vibes that come along with this negative thought cycle.

If someone did you wrong, don't let them invade more of your life by letting them live in your mind. *Let it go.*

Had a tough day? Don't let it carry on day after day. *Let it go.*

Life hasn't gone as planned? Well, it doesn't for anyone. *Let it go.*

Don't let these upsets linger for too long; they're taking up precious space. If you really want to create your best life, you have to learn how to shift your mind from the prison of your past. Focus on the good. Drop the negative stories and respond to life by giving your attention to what you can do today to get in a better position. If you don't let go of the heaviness from your past, your future will suffer, because what you do today builds your tomorrows.

Acceptance takes work. And it's not a one-time thing. You'll have to practice it every time your past is a greater focus than your present reality.

Sometimes it's an internal conversation that helps you let go of the negatives. But other times, you may need to actually talk it out. If that's the case, try having a *constructive venting session*. These are so darn good for the soul and the mind!

See, friend, if you bottle up negative emotions, then you're basically a ticking time bomb. That's why venting is actually a good thing. But there are two types of venting—the kind where you just complain and stew over details with hostility, and the kind where you get it all off your chest and then consider the possible solutions.

When you do this, you leave the darkness in the past so you can focus on the light of today and tomorrow. The past can't be any different. It is what it is. Accept what has happened to you and then choose, *How do I want to grow forward?*

THE MONK AND THE GIRL

This parable has been told God-knows-how-many times in front of audiences all over the world, so I'm not exactly sure where it originated, but it's a great illustration of carrying the past in your mind.

Here it goes…

Two monks are on a journey. In a village, they come across a young girl wearing a long kimono, trying to cross a muddy road without stepping into the mud. One monk picks her up, carries her across the road through the mud, and puts her down.

The monks walk on in silence for another four or five hours.

As they get close to their destination, the second monk says to the first, "You know, you shouldn't have done that. We monks aren't supposed to touch women, so you shouldn't have picked up that girl."

And the other monk says, "Oh, are you still carrying that girl? I put her down hours ago."

The one monk was still carrying the girl by replaying the event over and over in his head for hours. He was walking with this burden and was struggling with the reluctance of the human mind to let go of the past.

THE GIRL AND THE CURLS

I love that parable, but probably you're not a monk and chances are that you're not going to have to carry a girl across a muddy road anytime in the near future. But figuring out how to let go of the past? That's something each of us has to do every day, through huge life changes, minor hiccups, and daily disruptions.

In fact, it's those everyday frustrations that give us a chance to practice this skill. Let me give you an example.

I'm a curly girl, which means finding a really good stylist can be tricky. It takes a special combination of love, patience, talent, and knowledge to be really good at cutting curly hair, and when you find a magical stylist who has all of those attributes, you stay with them for the rest of your life.

Well, unless, like me, you move a thousand miles away from your old salon. In that case, when you realize you need a cut, you spend a month reading every review of every stylist within a fifty-mile radius of your new home.

All of a sudden, though, I was on a time crunch. I had a video project coming up for a client, and I wanted my hair to look good. So I took a leap of faith, swallowed down my nerves, and booked an appointment.

I won't take you through every gory detail, but let's just say the cut did not go as planned. I lost several inches of curls and left with my ends looking pretty uneven. But I was racing off to a speaking engagement and didn't even have time to process what was happening until later.

Let me tell you, it would've been really easy to stew in my bitter feelings. Just like that monk, I could've kept carrying the memory of that cut around with me. Instead, I gave myself permission to be upset, called my best friend and had a good vent sesh, and then decided that I was going to have to shift this internal narrative I was carrying around.

So I reflected on the lesson I needed to learn from the situation—trust your gut. I knew the cut wasn't going well. I voiced my concerns, but at the end of the day, I'd backed down and let her keep cutting because I didn't want to offend her. I made a mental note that the next time a moment like this popped up in my life, I needed to do what was best for me and not worry about how other people would take it, because their emotions are out of my control.

Then I decided that I had to stop replaying this situation in my head. What was done was done. Checking my hair in the mirror twenty-five times a day wasn't going to rewind time; it was just keeping me in the past. So every time I found myself walking toward the bathroom just to fuss at my ends, I physically stopped, turned around, and shifted my focus to my priorities for the day.

And I wrote myself a new story in my mind. I'd been telling myself, *My hair looks terrible. This is not what I wanted. I can't believe I lost four years of growth overnight.* But really, in spite of the fact that she'd taken off way too much, the shape wasn't terrible, and she hadn't left me with any crazy holes or a lopsided cut.

So I reframed that monologue that was running through my head. I told myself, *My hair is short. My curls are poppin' and healthy, so thankfully, they'll grow back.*

That's right. I just told you that I used *Stop & Shift* to work past a haircut.

If we want to be able to rely on our mind to conquer negative thoughts and carry us through the life-changing, earth-shattering, monumental moments, we've got to practice stopping and shifting our thoughts in the small disruptions we encounter every single day—a bad haircut, a traffic jam on the way to an appointment, a frustrating meeting with our boss, you name it.

Those are our opportunities to develop the mental agility we need to overcome every obstacle life throws in our path.

If you feel like you haven't been able to move forward, if you feel stuck or held back, then more than likely you're letting the baggage of your past distract you from building your future. You may not be able to change what's happened, but you can shape your tomorrows by choosing how you respond today.

GET IT ALL OUT

Write down things from the past you dwell on the most.

_____

_____

_____

_____

_____

_____

_____

How do you feel when these thoughts dominate your mind? Write down how you feel physically and how you feel emotionally.

_____

_____

_____

_____

_____

_____

_____

What details about this past experience do you need to accept?

_____

_____

_____

_____

_____

_____

_____

Are there any good qualities or lessons learned that you can carry with you from this experience?

_____

_____

_____

_____

_____

_____

_____

What's a happier scenario you can think about instead of ruminating about things that are out of your control?

_____

_____

_____

_____

_____

_____

_____

Is there a way to move forward? What would that look like?

_____

_____

_____

_____

_____

_____

_____

> **"** *Anxiety doesn't come from thinking about the future; it comes from wanting to control it.* **"**

10

Feeling Anxious

I can honestly say, I never experienced anxiety until I became an entrepreneur. And man, going through that increased my empathy for the folks who battle with anxiety disorders on a regular basis—it's no joke. That wave of panic can be debilitating.

Let me just note, this chapter is not addressing anxiety disorders (the main ones being generalized anxiety disorder or GAD, social anxiety disorder, panic disorder, separation anxiety disorder, and phobias). These are very serious disorders that can be caused by a number of factors like genetics, environment, or stressful or traumatic events in your life. Each type of anxiety disorder has its own treatment plan that should be talked through with a licensed professional.

But the fact still remains, we *all* experience anxiety.

Speaking in front of large groups can make you anxious. Driving in heavy traffic can be another common source of anxiety. The anticipation of a major meeting at work can also stir up rattled nerves.

Which is why practicing mindfulness is so gosh-darn important, because when it comes to speaking in front of that audience, it will help you find your calm. Or if you're in traffic, it will help you stay focused and alert. And when you're thinking about that meeting coming up, mindfulness will help you bring yourself back to the present moment, where you can simply do your best to prepare.

But there's one area of anxiety I want to address specifically while I have you here, because it's one I'm starting to see and hear about more and more from clients and friends. And that's living in the future.

Now, I just spent the whole last chapter telling you why it's dangerous to live in the past, but friend, there are also dangers involved in focusing too much on the future.

I don't know why our minds are hardwired to stay trapped in the past or live in the future, but that's why mental strength training is key to building a healthy and strong mindset. Exercises like *Stop & Shift* help rewire your thinking and create new grooves in your brain every time you repeat those healthy habits.

Yes, visualizing a future goal can definitely bring hope and give you a boost of energy to take action. But if you're not careful, you could lose sight of what's most important, where the real work needs to be done—the present. James Clear gives great advice on this in his book *Atomic Habits*. His mindshift came when he stopped focusing so much on the end goal and started focusing more on the systems, the processes, that he could put in place that would compound over time into a positive end result.[27] The only way to actually make progress, change your habits, and transform your life is to put effort into getting better day by day, in the present.

So, let's talk about the potential downside of spending too much time on the future. The short and simple answer is, living in the future can bring waves, or tsunamis, of anxiety. Think about the last time you felt anxious—what was it about? I bet you twenty bucks you were thinking about something in the future.

Let me reassure you, friend, this is totally normal!

Everyone experiences this because we're taught at a young age to plan ahead. Planning is okay; as a matter of fact, it's necessary to a certain extent. But anxiety kicks in when we feel like we have to *control* the future, which is impossible, hence the onset of distress.

Anxiety and worry are sometimes interchangeable, but they are slightly different. Worry is when you dwell on troubles and difficulties (this could be actual or potential problems). Anxiety is excessive fear or persistent worry, and it often refers to anticipation of future concern (feeling uneasy about something to come).

I learned this firsthand because of my ambitious heart and entrepreneurial spirit. I have *big* dreams—big, big dreams, y'all! But it's not the grandiose goals that give me angst; it's *how I'm going to get there*. I've come to realize that my anxiety is triggered when I get tripped up by details that are out of my control.

> Anxiety kicks in when we feel like we have to *control* the future.

And listen, feeling anxious is totally normal and, you could say, should be expected. But a lot of times, it's not the first wave of anxiety that's debilitating; it's *resisting* the anxious feelings that causes more anxiety! Our anxiety is heightened when we notice it and try to fight it.

Like I said earlier, anxiety can motivate us to prepare or practice, it can help us be more cautious, and it can even be a warning sign that we need to slow down and become more present.

HOW DO YOU MEASURE SUCCESS?

Here's an example of how anxiety can actually be a pretty powerful reminder that we need to check in with ourselves. I told you that even with everything I'd been through, I'd never really experienced anxiety until I became an entrepreneur. Entrepreneurship is a tough road. I absolutely love it, and it's brought so many joys and blessings into my life, but it's not easy.

As I mentioned earlier in this book, for the first few years I wasn't making the money I was hoping I would. There was no stability. I was working several consulting jobs just to continue to provide for our little family. There was no money for Caleb to do all of the extracurricular activities he wanted to do. Heck, I wouldn't even buy myself vitamins because that felt like a luxury item in our family budget. I could feel my energy dimming because I was so focused on not having a steady flow of income.

I finally reached a point where my anxiety forced me to ask myself why I was still doing this work. I was always worried about money, and honestly, I was discouraged. Why was I still taking this path?

And then I had a moment of clarity. I was seeing income as the only measure of my success. But my soul reminded me that that wasn't the main reason I had decided to become an entrepreneur.

See, after I'd lost my job, I'd realized that I had an opportunity to build a different life for me and Caleb.

I made the decision to start my own business because I wanted to have the flexibility to always be present for him. I knew that corporate America wasn't accommodating to single parents. And I was the only parent Caleb had; when he needed me, I didn't want there to be any question in his mind that I would show up for him.

Becoming an entrepreneur appealed to me because I wanted to have the freedom to be there for him. I didn't want to carry home someone else's expectations or stress; I needed to be able to create healthy boundaries around my work.

The anxiety about money actually forced me to slow down and revisit my "why." I was trying to define my success by the number of dollars in my bank account, and focusing so much on that one metric was out of alignment with my original goal.

So I shifted my perspective a bit as I looked at my story of success. Instead of focusing on my income, I turned my focus back to my original goal—creating a career and a lifestyle that allowed me to give Caleb what he needed. I asked myself, *Does he feel loved? Does he feel safe? Is he thriving? Does he have a loving, healthy, safe environment in which to grow?*

And you know what? I could answer *yes* to every single one of those questions. Maybe it didn't look the way I'd envisioned it, but at the end of the day, my business allowed me to be present for my son, which was what he most needed from me.

Money wasn't my endgame. The quality of our life together was the most important measure of my success. I was so focused on this one aspect of my business that I couldn't see that I was already living out the intention I'd set for myself.

That anxiety I was trying so hard to avoid and stuff down was really an opportunity to grow. When I recognized the negative feelings mounting, I stopped fighting and created space to let them flow—and as anxiety flowed out, equanimity flowed in. Practicing *Stop & Shift* in this moment allowed me to check in with myself, slow down, and reset my focus.

THE SECOND ARROW

It's when you try to fight against experiences in life, anxious moments included, that you're inducing more suffering.

Have you ever heard of the "second arrow" parable?

Buddha said, "In life, we cannot always control the first arrow. However, the second arrow is our reaction to the first. And with this second arrow comes the possibility of choice."

This is often summarized as, "Pain is inevitable, but suffering is optional."

Anxiety is inevitable, but when you allow yourself to flow with it instead of fighting against it, your mind will stay open to creative ways to handle this stress and tension. A few deep breaths can soothe your mind and help get oxygen and blood flow to the brain to create mental space.

I practice this all the time! I told you, I have really, really big goals—so big I really haven't told anyone about EVERYthing that's on my heart because I know some people will think I'm crazy.

One time, I opened up to one of my cousin-siblings. (In my family we're super close—closer than cousins—so we coined this term to more accurately define our relationship.) I told her all of my dreams, and when I finished, I said, "I know that all sounds crazy."

And her response not only surprised me, but it's stayed with me forever.

She said, "No, it's not. It's not like you said you were going to grow golden trees or something. Everything you just mentioned is something that someone else is doing, so why wouldn't you be able to? Of course you can! You can do anything."

I hugged her, cried a bit (told y'all I'm a crier), and thanked her for helping me adjust my perspective.

Are my goals big? Heck yes.

But are they attainable? Heck yes!

And whenever I feel anxious about my ambitious dreams, I release the pressure and perfection, I hold on to the excitement and joy it brings me, and I focus on the tasks I can control today that will help me build those dreams.

Would you like a sneak peek of a page from my dream journal, friend? Okay, shhh, don't tell anyone else...

I want to help change lives all around the world. I surrender to being a vessel of hope and courage to inspire others.

If I'm being totally real here, I have big, big dreams to live out my purpose.

I want to put on wellness conferences, but not like your typical conference. These are going to feel good all the way to your soul. And breakout sessions that aren't just PowerPoints; they will be fun, hands-on learning experiences to help the audience see and feel tangible results in a matter of minutes.

We'll cover everything from the big life-changing events like death, divorce, losing a job, becoming a caregiver, long-term illness diagnosis, to the smaller stressors like parenting, navigating toxic relationships, and common internal battles.

I want these conferences to be truly life-changing! A space where vulnerability is met with actionable takeaways and strengthened by community and connection.

I also want to co-host retreats with other experts and coaches, held all over the world! The participants will be fully immersed in mental, physical, emotional, and spiritual goodness. Learning, activities, and even built-in rest time will give them the reset experience they were looking for with lifelong habits to take back with them.

How cool would it be to work with humans around the world who are breaking through social norms, who are on fire to live out their purpose, who are bold leaders who want to keep their head in the game to be their best at home, at work, and just in life overall. Man, that energy would be ahhhhmazing!

And last, but most definitely not least—I want to be an international keynote speaker and travel all around the world with my son. I want to share what I've learned in life as a widow, an entrepreneur, a single mom, a student of life, and a goal-getter. If my life experiences can help someone else, that would be such a blessing. And for Caleb to experience it all with me is the ultimate goal. I don't ever want him to feel the strife of a single-parent income, and I want him to experience all this world has to offer. Most of all, I want him to see his mom take something bad and do something good with it.

This is my ultimate dream.

Dang, it felt good to get that out.

I realize that I can't control the future, but I can 100% control my effort today. Yes, I have huge dreams, but I'm also working my butt off to build them. My sleeves are rolled up. I have scrapes and bruises from all the missed steps. I'm grinding—hard. And in the midst of the daily duties, yes, I battle the anxiety that comes along with it.

Those defeating thoughts like:

Will I ever fulfill all of these dreams?

Will I be able to live up to the promise I made myself about the life I want to create for my son?

How do I go further faster?

How do I help and reach more people?

And here's the biggest one—*am I doing enough today to get to where I want to be?*

If I could describe my mind when it's overthrown with anxiety, it would be like standing on the subway platform in NYC as a train is flying into the station. The loud sound the wind creates, mixed with the screeching of the wheels on the tracks, while the windows, doors, and people fly by. But with anxiety, the train never stops.

I've learned that the only way to make it stop is to shift from looking at the train (rapid thoughts) to looking down at your feet (where you are at this moment).

One of my favorite books of all time, which taught me how to manage my anxiety as an entrepreneur, is *The One Thing* by Gary Keller. And best of all, the principles he teaches also translate to life outside of business. One of the most impactful quotes from the book is, "What you build today will either empower or restrict your tomorrow."[28] This is so true, and it also applies to your mindset.

Now, while our situations are probably very different, anxiety about the future is the same for all of us. Not knowing what's to come is a struggle everyone faces in some way, shape, or form. Heck, have you ever been anxious before a flight? Anxious about getting married or having kids? Anxious about starting a new job?

Remember, all of this is normal. But when you become consumed with fear and unable to live in the moment, it can be unhealthy or even dangerous.

Yes, planning for the future is a very responsible thing to do, but when you notice your emotions turning down Anxiety Lane, use that as an opportunity to practice shifting your mindset and bringing yourself back to the present. Every time you do this, your brain is getting stronger.

One day I shared this metaphor with a client, and she found it helpful because it's so dang relatable and it paints a really simple picture of how to take action when you're feeling anxious about something. So I promised I'd include it in this book.

ONE SOCK AT A TIME

You know that one room in your house that needs to be cleaned? Or that messy closet that needs to be organized? Or your garage that needs to be cleared out because you have a bunch of junk that's piled up and is not being used?

Or, okay, here's one I'm sure *everyone* (except my mom) can relate to—the pile of clean laundry that needs to be folded and/or put away.

Yeah, you know the one; it's been there for like TWO WEEKS, and it's growing! (If you can't relate to this, then please reserve your judgment for someone else—because this is a real problem for some of us!)

Anxiety can be an immediate emotional response when you're at the starting point of any major project—whether it's a two-week pile of laundry, a messy room, planning a trip, or buying a home.

When you're looking ahead and start to feel anxious about getting to that destination, I like to say, *just start folding one sock at a time.* Every time I look at a pile of laundry, if I feel overwhelmed, I put it off, and the pile grows. Eventually, it turns into a monster pile.

Finally, when Caleb and I are down to our last pair of socks or underwear and I know I can't ignore it any longer, I have to muster up the energy and focus to get it done.

By this time, it's not only the task, it's the amount of laundry that needs to be folded and put away that brings me grief. But instead of proclaiming, "This stresses me out," I tell myself, "Just one piece of clothing at a time."

Before I know it, the pile is shrinking, there's light at the end of the tunnel, and my anxiety is melting away. Why? Because I took action by focusing on one thing at a time.

Guys, I'm telling you! This train of thinking works for *everything in life.*

> Train your brain not to live in the future for too long so you can be productive in the present.

Sometimes you just need to interrupt the overwhelm of anxiety by asking yourself, *What is the one thing I can do right now that will make everything easier?* Or, *what's the one thing I can do right now that will lead me to the goal?* Or, *what's the one thing I can control right now, in this moment?*

Maybe it's a task to get done. Or maybe it's focusing on your breathing to stay calm. Either way, bring yourself back to the one thing you can do at this very moment. Train your brain not to live in the future for too long so you can be productive in the present.

To quote my guy Gary again, "Success requires action, and action requires thought."[29]

I have an exercise at the end of this chapter to help you think about your biggest source of anxiety and then identify what's most important today. Life gets clearer and less complicated when you focus on one task at a time. The better we manage our thoughts, the less anxious we will feel about future details and major milestones.

ONE SOCK AT A TIME

If there's anything on the horizon that's making you nervous, write that below.

_____

_____

_____

_____

_____

_____

_____

_____

_____

_____

Next, write down the details that replay in your head that are causing anxiety.

_____

_____

_____

_____

_____

_____

_____

_____

_____

_____

_____

Finally, write down the most important task in this very moment that will lead you to that milestone.

_____

_____

_____

_____

_____

_____

_____

_____

_____

_____

_____

11

Neglecting Your Needs

Ohhhh man, this right here is about to be my favorite chapter to write.

Seriously, friend, of all the life lessons I had to learn during my darkest times, the importance of taking care of myself was the biggest, most impactful one of all. It's at the heart of all the disciplines I mentioned previously.

When you see yourself as a priority and when you are committed to taking care of *your* needs, the rest becomes much easier. I mean, let's be real, if it wasn't about your needs, you wouldn't even be reading this book. You know you need to do a better job of taking care of you, and I'm here to affirm—YES YOU DO.

I don't care what anyone says…you have to take care of you first—and regularly—otherwise you'll have nothing to give to others. I once heard it said, "What benefits you benefits those around you."

Before self-care was a hot topic and trending Pinterest board, it was my pathway back to a whole heart, which is why, in this chapter, I want to dive into the importance of taking care of yourself mentally, physically, emotionally, spiritually, and socially, because no one knows your needs better than you do.

Let me tell you about the pivotal moment in my healing journey when I realized this truth. About two months after Richard died, I went to my physician looking for a "happy pill," something to help lift the fog that had my mind confused, anxious, and clouded with complicated emotions.

I didn't know what to expect. I'd never had the need for antidepressants or anxiety meds, so my understanding of them was limited. The doctor knew of my situation. I mean, who didn't? It was all over the news.

But still, she went through the standard questions to gauge my mental state. After only a few minutes, she handed me a Rx for a couple of medications, told me to call her if my thoughts became suicidal, and sent me on my way. My friend took me to get the scripts filled, and when I arrived home, I went straight to my bathroom, placed the bottles on the counter, sat on my little bench with my chin on the countertop, and started bawling.

Is this what my life had come to? I had to rely on meds because I couldn't get myself together?

Before someone tries to come for me, let me say this loud and clear: this isn't a knock against people who do need medication. I just never struggled with anything like this, so in that moment, I felt hopeless and was frustrated with my inability to "bounce back" or to get any kind of professional help beyond a pill.

Two or three days later, after being a zombie and barely getting out of bed, my little one (who was two years old at the time), walked into my room and said, "Mommy, are you going to get up today? Are you going to eat?"

I don't know what it was about those words that triggered something new inside of me. His words pierced my heart and opened my mind. It was in that moment that I realized I had two choices: I could either give up or get up.

"Yes, baby," I said. "Mommy will be down in a minute." I slid out of bed, walked into the bathroom, and flushed the pills down the toilet.

I looked at myself in the mirror and gave myself the pep talk I needed:

You can do this. You will do this. Even if you can't find the strength or willpower to do it for yourself, do it for Caleb. He needs you to be a whole, healthy, happy mommy.

No one is here to pick you up. No one else understands what you're going through. And no one else can take care of your needs. There's no quick fix, and no one is coming to save you—so let's just take it one breath at a time.

From that moment on, I committed to taking responsibility for my healing because it hit me like a zap of lightning: if I don't take care of myself, how will I be able to take care of my child? I could hear the flight attendants over the PA in my head: "In case of an emergency, put your oxygen mask on first before assisting others." What a great metaphor for life.

Self-care isn't selfish.

One more time, a little louder for the folks in the back: self-care isn't selfish. It's self-love, and most of all, it's *necessary*.

I heard it once said, "Self-care is giving the world the best of you, instead of what's left of you." (Haha, pulled that one from good ol' Pinterest!) Think about it—no one knows your needs better than you. And no one can tell you what is best for you, because it's impossible for them to fully understand the inner workings of your body, mind, and soul. Just like you can't fully understand theirs.

Speaking of body, mind, and soul, when I talk about self-care, I am referring to your *whole* self. Not just pampering your body with facials, massages, and yummy-scented oils—you have to care for your entire well-being, because everything is intertwined. Even the most basic self-care practice—like drinking water, for example—isn't necessary just because water is good for your body, but also because it helps your brain function properly.

And going for a walk—yes, it's good for the body, but it's also so good for the mind and soul to be outdoors. Now, don't get all stressed or bent out of shape trying to devise an elaborate self-care plan. Keep it simple; start with one or two habits. When I started paying more attention to my total well-being, I began with little habits like these:

- Drink water all day.
- Eat more fruits and vegetables, less sugar.
- Get more sleep—go to bed earlier.
- Go for a walk or play outside with Caleb.
- Pray and meditate daily.

Friend, these are really simple and easy habits that anyone can do. I set the bar low because I knew I was starting from a depleted place. You'd be surprised how small adjustments can make a huge impact on your energy, your focus, and your overall health. And if you still don't see how all of these areas connect, I know you'll be able to relate to this more common scenario…

WATCH OUT, MAMA'S HANGRY!

When was the last time you crossed over from hungry to hangry?

Here's a likely scenario: After dropping the kids off at school in the morning, the only thing that stands between you and your first item on your to-do list is a cup of coffee. Once you get the fuel you need to get your day started, it's off to the races.

You answer the emails, pay the bills, hop on a conference call, work on a few outstanding items, maybe even start a load of laundry…before you know it, it's time to pick up the kids from school.

On your way there, you realize you missed breakfast—and lunch—and that midday granola bar isn't doing diddly-squat for your energy level.

The kids pile in the car, and they are chatty!

They want to tell you everything that happened that day. How someone pushed them to cut the line at the water fountain. The new book they got at the library. Asking for the hundredth time that week if you organized a playdate with their friends; if not, then when will you text their mom? Oh, and what's for dinner?

Oh, shoot! Dinner!

You totally forgot to take something out of the freezer for dinner, and now you've officially hit your max. As your frustration seeps in, the next question rolls out of your sweet kiddo's mouth, and without intending to do so, you lose it!

What happened? You forgot to take care of yourself all day.

You neglected your well-being (unintentionally…you were hyperfocused on crushing your to-do list), and now the side effects are in full effect.

Here's a shift meant for earlier in the day to help prevent hangry mood swings: When you are powering through your to-do list, at some point you will notice that you need to eat, but you just choose not to stop and ignore the first sign. In that moment, honor your body. Instead of telling yourself, *I don't have time to stop and eat because I'm too busy with work and everything else,* remind yourself, *My health always comes first. I will achieve twice as much in half the time thanks to my energy and mental performance.*

If you find yourself in the midst of a hangry moment, even if it's after a snap at your kiddos or your partner, it's okay to atone for your behavior with an apology and the truth: "I'm sorry. My crankiness is because I didn't give my body what it needed today. How about we grab something healthy to eat so I can refuel?"

That's one example that almost everyone can relate to. But here's the thing—self-care comes in many forms: managing your time on technology, setting healthy boundaries with toxic people, exercising or moving your body, eating healthy, enjoying new experiences, and definitely resting and having some downtime.

For far too long, we've been programmed to believe that everything and everyone else is more important than caring for our personal needs, but that is absolutely not true. If you don't take care of yourself, you'll have nothing left to give to those you love. And not to mention, you're going to be running on fumes and feeling depleted.

Think about it this way: When you take care of yourself, you can bring your best self to the table in your interactions. You can be present in the moment when the people you love need you. Self-care allows you to cultivate your own inner peace, which gives you the space to respond to other people in a genuine and loving way. So when I tell you that self-care isn't selfish, I really mean it. Self-care is the foundation you need to be able to bring the strength, confidence, and calm necessary to nurture or support anyone else.

Okay, let's make a plan. I've included an activity for you at the end of this chapter to help you brainstorm self-care activities that you can easily integrate into your daily routine. And to make sure you're covering all the bases, I've broken it down into the four traditional areas of wellness: mental, emotional, physical, and spiritual.

I'm not asking you to make huge adjustments or sacrifices. Honestly, small changes can make a big impact. But we do want to make sure we're hitting all areas of our total well-being so we can be in harmony.

THE RIPPLE EFFECT

Personal growth is a journey that will last a lifetime, and self-care is one of the many elements of this journey. But the more you know yourself, love yourself, and trust yourself, the more you grow into the fullness of who you were created to be!

To know yourself means to be aware of who you are today and the person you want to become. If there are parts you don't like, that's okay; you've got to admit that even the no-so-great parts exist until you change them—otherwise, you'll never change. Challenge your fears so they don't block your greatness. And check in with your motivations, because when you operate with a clean heart, you'll always win. Get to know yourself, and set an internal standard for who you want to be.

> The most important relationship to invest in is the one with yourself.

Loving yourself is expressed in many ways, like showing self-compassion and giving yourself grace. Also, speak kindly to yourself instead of letting automatic negative self-talk dominate your mind. And don't overlook the simple acts of love, like listening to good music, going on a walk, taking a nap, doing some deep breathing, or rolling around on the floor and stretching. We tend to invest so much in external relationships, when really, the most important relationship to invest in is the one with yourself.

And then finally, trusting yourself means being secure and unwavering about who you want to be and allowing your inner guide to help you make the best decisions along the way. Honor yourself. If something doesn't feel good, walk away or say "no." Speak up for yourself—even in the smallest of ways. When you speak up for yourself in small ways, you'll find it easier to speak up for yourself in big ways too. Learn to listen to the calm, peaceful voice inside you. Surrender to the journey and trust yourself to do what you can while other pieces fall into place. You don't have to know every detail about how it will all work; you just have to begin to open up to the idea that it will.

Neglecting your needs is a disservice to yourself and the world, because what benefits you, directly and indirectly, benefits those around you. When you become better, you make the people around you better, and the world a little better too. That's the glorious ripple effect of personal growth. So stop putting yourself on the back burner and give yourself permission to step into your whole, amazing self! No matter the detours or obstacles that may try to take you off course, when you know, love, and trust yourself, your inner guide will always help you find your way back.

In the space below, brainstorm different habits and activities that would benefit each area of your total well-being. You can research activities online (I enjoy browsing Pinterest for "self-care ideas"). You'll find that some activities can serve more than one area, which is great!

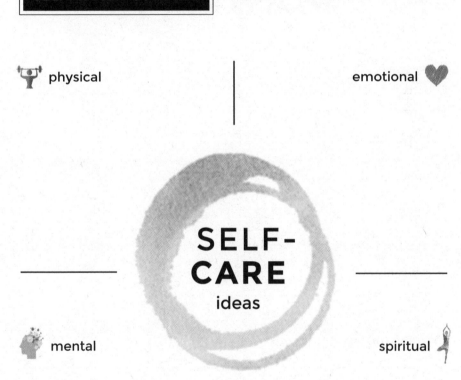

Now in the space below, select three habits from the previous page and write them next to the corresponding area of well-being. From there, take ONE of those habits and write it into your day—either morning, afternoon, or evening. This is how you integrate self-care into your day in a practical way instead of making it an every-once-in-a-while occurrence.

MY ACTION PLAN

physical

emotional

mental

spiritual

morning routine

_____

_____

_____

_____

afternoon routine

_____

_____

_____

_____

evening routine

_____
_____
_____
_____

MEALS

breakfast

_____
_____
_____
_____

lunch

_____
_____
_____
_____

dinner

_____
_____
_____
_____

" You either control your mind, or it controls you. "

12

Finding Flow

"A bird sitting on a branch is never afraid of the branch breaking, because the belief is not in the strength of the branch but the strength in her own wings" (anonymous). That's definitely worth highlighting. What a beautiful reminder that everything you need is already inside of you.

I may not know you or your circumstances, but I do know that the human mind is a powerful tool—and you have access to it. Finding yourself in a negative thought cycle and hitting the brakes on that downward spiral is an incredible strength that all of us have. Most of us just don't tap into it.

If I could give you one gift, it would be the ability to recognize how capable you already are. Remember when I told you at the start that I know *Stop & Shift* can change your life? That wasn't just about my confidence in my own method. It's also because I also know without a doubt in my mind that the capacity to transform your thought patterns lives within you. You are a force.

Negative thinking can progressively lead to more unhealthy thought patterns and habits as time goes on. But the reverse is also true: positive thinking leads to positive living. You must cling to the positive. Mindset tools, like *Stop & Shift*, help you tap into your mental potential so you can climb out of the downward spiral and start a new cycle of strength. This is the beginning of transforming your mind.

> Positive thinking leads to positive living.

I'm not saying being positive always makes things better, but being negative always makes things worse. Your ability to bounce back from setbacks and gently pull yourself out of negative thought loops, all while holding on to hope and growing forward, is what I like to call *flow*.

Life will be hard at times; we can't avoid that. So when hard times find you, learn to flow and not force. Your challenge isn't avoiding negative feelings. It's learning to surf each wave and find calm waters again. Allow those events to take their course, give yourself permission to have a good cry, learn from them, and accept that some things cannot be explained. This release of energy is so cleansing for your body and soul and will keep you in flow.

Your job is to make good choices that create the right conditions for you to flourish. The struggles that cause you pain are doorways to awareness, healing, and growth. Have the courage to dive into your uncomfortable feelings so you can gently and compassionately explore them.

When you flow, you're always in a position to take your power back.

That's why it's important to practice this mental exercise daily. When you do, you'll develop a mindset that isn't fixated on and limited by the negative noise; instead it's buoyant and flows with the information and scenarios it encounters. The biggest mental flex is when nothing can affect your inner peace without your conscious permission. You'll be able to identify a negative thought pattern, stop it in its tracks, and interject truth.

The big question you may be left wondering is, *Will the negative thoughts ever stop?*

Unfortunately, the answer is no. There's no trick or method to prevent stressful thoughts from entering the mind. But that's just one more mindset shift we each have the power to make. Remind yourself that the goal isn't to get rid of negative thoughts. That's literally impossible if you are a human living in this world. What is possible is changing your response to those thoughts.

And that's the ultimate goal. To grow so strong that you can make space in your mind to watch those negative thoughts instead of being entangled in them, and then choose how you're going to show up in the present moment. And there's one thing you can be sure of—your growth will always be tested. So use every tough moment, setback, and toxic thought as an opportunity to practice the skills you've learned. Flowing in small disruptions is great habit formation that prepares your mind for when the big life events unfold.

What does this look like in real time?

Well, remember that evening I had a stressful breakdown on the way to a networking event? Around that time, I'd applied for nearly one hundred speaking engagements. One was a mega women's conference, BlogHer. It was the first conference I attended as a newbie-entrepreneur, and the energy was so inspiring, I wanted to bring an empowering message back to their audience. And that year it was actually being held where I lived in Orlando! Out of all the engagements I'd applied for, I wanted this one more than anything.

Several weeks went by. Then, at the end of February, I received an email: "There were so many applications. Thanks for submitting, but you weren't selected."

My heart dropped. I was so bummed. But then, after a brief moment, I shifted my thoughts from the woe-is-me story to "Welp, there must be something else I'm supposed to be doing that weekend. If this door was closed, that's because another is going to open."

I deleted the email and went on with my day.

Now, I could've stayed stuck in sadness. I could've sat and cried my eyes out (you know I'm no stranger to bawling). But instead, I decided to accept the decision that had been made and press on. I chose not to dwell on it. I reframed my thoughts to something positive. I made a conscious choice not to let this rejection letter ruin my day and committed to opening myself up to the other opportunities that might present themselves. That's how *Stop & Shift* helps you flow.

Want to know something pretty amazing? There *was* something else coming down my path scheduled for the same dates. A few weeks after being rejected by BlogHer, I was formally invited to do a TEDx talk, which was being held the same weekend as the conference.

Flow happens when you roll with the inevitable ups and downs that life brings. Stuff is going to happen; that's life. And it shouldn't surprise us when things don't work out all peachy-keen. The unexpected hardships, rejection, stank-attitude people, spilled coffee, missed opportunities—unfortunately, it's all a part of life. This world is full of pain and disappointment, which is why managing your mind is necessary to preserve your peace and sanity.

Use those bumps in the road as opportunities to flex your mental strength and grow with the flow. You're gonna get through this life one way or another. You get to choose whether you do it with a fixed, negative, and limiting mindset, or with the mental agility that opens your mind to positive energy, endless possibilities, and new opportunities.

I hope you feel empowered to choose the latter.

When everything feels out of control, you now have a powerful, life-changing tool that can help you calmly focus on your thoughts and choose a positive, productive response. The more you practice this, the less you'll feel hopeless or stuck, because you've discovered the secret: when you master your mind, you master your life.

10 TIPS TO MASTER YOUR MIND

If you're determined to grow, then you know it takes more than a few self-help books or listening to a guided meditation every now and again. It has to become a lifestyle. You get out what you put in, so if you really want to thrive through hard times and feel fully alive, then create an environment that helps you flourish. To help you do this, I'm going to leave you with my top 10 go-to tips from my personal toolbox.

1. **Practice *Stop & Shift* every day**—in the little moments and the big ones. Before you know it, it will become second nature and you will feel calm and centered in every situation.

2. **Establish good brain hygiene habits** like drinking water, getting enough sleep, and eating foods (or taking supplements) that support brain function. Take care of your brain; it's the only one you have!

3. **Surround yourself with people whose self-respect, self-worth, and values inspire you to elevate your own behavior.** Your peer circle directly influences your quality of life, so make sure to spend time with people who honor your needs and support your life goals.

4. **Meditate regularly to create more space inside.** Even if you can only meditate for three to five minutes a day, that's better than zero minutes. The benefits of meditation are surprisingly abundant and impact all areas of your well-being.

5. **Take mindful breaks during the workday**—breaks are not a luxury. If you want to perform at your best, you have to honor your brain's natural rhythm of rest. Otherwise you'll push yourself beyond your limits and your output will fall short.

6. **Try something new that takes you slightly outside of your comfort zone.** Go to a dance class, hike a mountain trail, take surf lessons. Healthy risks help you grow, evolve, and have fun.

7. **Read.** Books take you to new places and open your mind with new information. Rotate between fiction and nonfiction to really keep your mind sharp and in expansion mode.

8. **Laugh**—every day. Laughter is good for the mind and the soul, and we should be more intentional about bringing joy into our lives. You can watch cute puppies on TikTok or videos from your favorite comedian. Personally, I tickle my son every night at bedtime to make sure we both laugh at least once a day.

9. **Soak up the sun.** Sitting in the sunlight for a few minutes feels like a warm hug from the Creator of the Universe. Even if I'm out for a walk, at some point I'll stand or sit for a couple of minutes with my eyes closed to appreciate the sun's radiant energy.

10. **Sprinkle kindness everywhere.** This can happen in so many ways: a random act of generosity, a compliment, or even showing appreciation. Kindness goes a long way; it's an energy exchange that benefits both the receiver and the giver.

Mindset is everything. Your life begins inside your mind, and the thoughts you let linger will shape everything your life touches. Where you are right now might feel comfortable, but where you could be is absolutely amazing. This is your chance to begin again, friend, to start something new today. And let me tell you, life always offers a beautiful new beginning to anyone brave enough to reach for it.

Here's to a new day, a new chapter in your life, and a new mindset. If you're ready to commit to a new way of thinking, I encourage you to cut out the last page of this chapter and post it somewhere where you'll see it every day.

You are brave, bold, and more capable than you think!! You got this. I got this. We got this.

Big love,
Karen

BONUS: As my gift to you, get all the tools and exercises in this book, plus additional free content, as a download at https://www.karenallen.co/stop-and-shift

I, _____, on this day, _____
_____, 20____, commit to choosing a new way of thinking.

I will release negative thoughts and reframe my worries, anxieties, and fears to serve my growth. I will keep my heart anchored in gratitude by focusing on all the good I have in my life instead of focusing on what I don't have or what's wrong.

The following negative thoughts are no longer welcome in my mind:

_____
_____
_____
_____

Whenever I feel overwhelmed by a negative thought, I will practice the following healthy habits:

_____
_____
_____
_____

I accept that I'm not perfect, and life isn't perfect, but that won't stop me from being my best. My thoughts are not my identity. My thoughts don't control my actions. I control my thoughts. I won't fight with my thoughts, I will let them flow and then choose the best one that will bring a positive outcome. I will give myself grace while I grow, and when I fall off course, I will find my way back to center by honoring the values of a clean heart. Those values are love, peace, patience, kindness, goodness, faithfulness, and self-control.

I take full responsibility for my thoughts and will choose them wisely. I am the master of my mind.

_____

(Your signature)

NOTES

1. Joan Podrazik, "'Be Responsible for Your Own Life,' Says Oprah (VIDEO)," *Huffpost*, last updated December 31, 2012, https://www.huffpost.com/entry/be-responsible-take-responsibility-oprah_n_2330820.
2. R. G. Tedeschi and L. G. Calhoun, "The Posttraumatic Growth Inventory: Measuring the Positive Legacy of Trauma," *Journal of Traumatic Stress* 9, no. 3 (July 1996): 455–71, doi: 10.1007/BF02103658.
3. Sheryl Sandberg and Adam Grant, *Option B: Facing Adversity, Building Resilience, and Finding Joy* (New York: Alfred A. Knopf, 2017), 12.
4. "Mindfulness," *Merriam-Webster*, Merriam-Webster, Inc., n.d., https://www.merriam-webster.com/dictionary/mindfulness.
5. "Mindfulness," *Wikipedia*, Wikimedia Foundation, last updated February 12, 2022, https://en.wikipedia.org/wiki/Mindfulness.
6. "OPTIMIZE with Brian Johnson," YouTube video, June 10, 2015, https://www.youtube.com/watch?v=j78AjMIIHLo&feature=youtu.be.
7. @TheQuoteBibles, "Why Waste Time," *TikTok*, May 23, 2021, https://www.tiktok.com/foryou?is_from_webapp=v1&item_id=6965601614375718150#/@thequotebibles/video/6965601614375718150.
8. Rob Dupe, "How Small Changes Can Help You Build and Upward Spiral," *Forbes*, October 30, 2021, https://www.forbes.com/sites/robdube/2021/10/30/how-small-changes-can-help-you-build-an-upward-spiral/?sh=2131efff1dbf.
9. Caroline Leaf, *Switch On Your Brain: The Key to Peak Happiness, Thinking, and Health* (Grand Rapids, MI: BakerBooks, 2013), 45, 61.
10. Ibid., 34.
11. Ibid., 207, n. 4.
12. Cover copy, *Switch On Your Brain: The Key to Peak Happiness, Thinking, and Health* (Grand Rapids, MI: BakerBooks, 2013).
13. Carol Dweck, *Mindset: The New Psychology of Success* (Ballantine Books, 2006 [2016]), 7.
14. Ibid., emphasis mine.
15. Ibid., 38.
16. "Mind Matters: How to Create More Positive Thoughts," TLEX Institute, n.d., https://tlexinstitute.com/how-to-effortlessly-have-more-positive-thoughts/.
17. "When I Look Back on All the Worries," *Quotes.net*, STANDS4, LLC, n.d., https://www.quotes.net/quote/11925.
18. Lucas S. LaFreniere and Michelle G. Newman, "Exposing Worry's Deceit: Percentage of Untrue Worries in Generalized Anxiety Disorder Treatment," *Behavioral Therapy* 51, no. 3 (May 2020): 413–23, doi: 10.1016/j.beth.2019.07.003.

19. Michael Singer, *The Untethered Soul: The Journey Beyond Yourself* (Oakland, CA: Noetic Books, 2007), 11.

20. Markham Heid, "You Asked: Is It Bad for You to Read the News Constantly?" *TIME Magazine*, last updated May 19, 2020, https://time.com/5125894/is-reading-news-bad-for-you/.

21. Paulo Coelho, *The Alchemist*, 25th anniversary ed. (New York: HarperOne, 1988), 29.

22. Stephen Cope, *The Great Work: A Guide for the Journey Toward Your True Calling* (New York: Bantam Books, 2015).

23. "Ikigai," *Oxford English Dictionary*, Oxford University Press, retrieved July 24, 2021, https://www.oed.com/view/Entry/74433529.

24. Cope, *Great Work*, 23.

25. "17 Dolly Parton Quotes on Success That Will Inspire You," *Southern Living Magazine*, n.d., https://www.southernliving.com/culture/dolly-parton-quotes-success.

26. Nick Vujicic, "Overcoming Hopelessness," TEDxNoviSad, YouTube video, 14:53, September 15, 2015, https://www.youtube.com/watch?v=0YBJC0b6mWE.

27. James Clear, *Atomic Habits: An Easy & Proven Way to Build Good Habits & Break Bad Ones* (New York: Avery, 2018).

28. Gary Keller, *The One Thing: The Surprisingly Simple Truth Behind Extraordinary Results* (London: John Murray Press, 2001), 89.

29. Ibid., 87.

ACKNOWLEDGMENTS

There are so many wonderful people I want to thank for their impact on my life. Because of them, I am the person I am today as I sit here writing these pages. I'm afraid it might sound like I'm giving a speech at the Grammys, but I really don't care because this book carries the love, light, and lessons I've absorbed from each of them.

First, to my late husband, Richard. I wish you could see your name in this book and know how much my growth has been inspired by your transformation. I can imagine your big smile and hear your enthusiastic, hype-man voice saying, "You did that, babe." I miss you.

Caleb—my cub—thank you for your love; it carried me through my worst days. Parenting is the best place to practice *Stop & Shift*, so I owe you a world of thanks for all of the hours of training! Most of all, when you notice I'm stressed or overwhelmed, thank you for gently reminding me of the mindful habits I preach to you.

Mom and Dad, I know without a doubt that my strength and grit come from your superhuman DNA. Thank you for your unconditional love and support, for staying so close when I fell apart, and for holding me down while I rebuilt.

Jenny, you've been in my corner since I was born. From prying the casts off my infant legs to opening your home to me and Caleb, and all of the coffee dates since then, your love and support have become a firm foundation that anchors me.

Chris & Ash—the truest best friends a girl could ever ask for. No matter the time apart or distance between us, I've always felt the comfort of your unwavering love over the decades. Whether I was in the pits of the hell of middle school, widowhood, or entrepreneurship, you've been with me through it all. I freakin' love y'all.

Taryn—welp, all of the cheesy Pinterest quotes are true: a soulmate isn't always a romantic partner; sometimes it's your bestie. Thank you for every moment, every call, every prayer, and every tear we've shared. Your friendship is one of my favorite #GodHugs of all time.

Nina, my cousin-sibling who told me growing golden trees would be a ridiculous aspiration but everything else is possible—thank you for helping me believe in my big, bold dreams.

To the team who surrounds this work…
Jackie, you helped me find my voice and for that I'm forever grateful.

Melissa, thank you for believing in me from the very beginning and for everything you do to help me take this message far and wide.

Simon, from the first time we met you generously poured your wisdom into me, opened doors to new opportunities, and encouraged me in all of my endeavors. Thank you for saying yes to coffee.

Dave and Jen, thank you for not only believing in this book, but for bringing it to life! The entire Sound Wisdom family has been an incredible blessing and joy to work with.

Jayne, you helped me bring 100% Human™ to the world, dig deep to discover my soul work, and reconnect to my inner guide. From our first meeting I knew our souls were meant to do good together. Lots of love.

AUTHOR BIO

Karen Allen is a TEDx speaker, the founder of 100% Human™ community, and a thought leader in the areas of mental wellness and personal growth. She is passionate about providing tools and resources to help individuals explore their potential and achieve their goals with a strong, healthy mindset.

Karen began her career in human resources and talent acquisition, leading countless training sessions, new processes, and change initiatives. However, at a young age, she suddenly became a widow when her husband was tragically murdered.

On the quest to rebuild her life, she discovered healthy habits and lifestyle changes that helped her find her way back to a whole heart and strong mind. Now, she shares practical advice and life strategies that provide tangible results and skills—including her highly acclaimed *Stop & Shift* mental strength training program—to help people develop a growth mindset so they can overcome the everyday challenges we all face in life and work.

Karen's client list includes YouTube, NBC's Golf Channel, HubSpot, told*right*, Universal Orlando Parks & Resorts, Kaiser Permanente, Leukemia & Lymphoma Society, AT&T, and many more! Her work has been featured in *Forbes* and *The Washington Post*, as well as on *Good Morning America*, MSNBC, and many other media outlets and podcasts.

For more resources on how to *Stop & Shift*,
please visit karenallen.co.

Book Karen for your next event:
http://www.karenallen.co/speaking.

Connect with Karen:

in http://www.linkedin.com/in/karenallenmillsap/

♪ http://www.tiktok.com/@karen.m.allen

◎ http://www.instagram.com/karen.m.allen/

ORDER YOUR COPY OF *STOP & SHIFT*